YOU, _____, WILL FIND

THE LIFT UP YOU NEED TO GO UP.

Life
Zig Ziglar's
Lifters

Zig Ziglar's Life Lifters

Moments of Inspiration for Living Life Better

ZIG ZIGLAR

BROADMAN
&HOLMAN
PUBLISHERS

Nashville, Tennessee

0–8054–2689–2

Published by Broadman & Holman Publishers
Nashville, Tennessee

Dewey Decimal Classification: 248.84
Subject Heading: ENCOURAGEMENT \
CHRISTIAN LIFE

1 2 3 4 5 6 7 8 9 10 07 06 05 04 03

Dedicated to the brave men and women—past, present, and future in our military forces—who have committed their lives to protect our faith, freedom, and families.

CONTENTS

ACKNOWLEDGMENTS

As always, when a work of this nature is completed, if we're going to be fair and honest we must admit that it was not a single effort. It's very much like when you see a turtle on a fence post. You can rest assured he didn't get there by himself! That's certainly true of this effort.

My acknowledgments begin with my beautiful redheaded wife Jean, who, as always, is my constant source of encouragement and who does the things for me that I not only hate to do, but am, in most cases, incapable of doing. Without her, the reading, research, and writing would have taken considerably longer.

My faithful executive assistant for these last twenty-five years, Laurie Magers, kept me organized through this effort as she helped me keep up with my other writing projects in the midst of her own hectic schedule. Her coordination of my speaking engagements and writing commitments is invaluable, and the way she and Julie bring everything together via phone, fax, and E-mail is awesome to me.

Julie Norman, my youngest daughter and the editor of my books and newspaper columns, is a strong guiding force as she brings a completely different dimension to what I do. I do most of the creative writing. But being female and of a different generation, Julie beautifully rounds off the rough edges, adds her feminine touch, and makes the writing more effective and far more palatable. In addition, she's just fun to work with and has a great attitude—a constant encouragement to me.

There are also those world-renowned writers, Mr. and Ms. Anonymous, who add significantly to my warehouse of information, facts, humor, human interest, etc. In addition, I must thank the media, particularly the print media, which frequently provides informative material as well as viable suggestions that are helpful to me when I put all of it together. And to those people, both known and unknown, who have encouraged me and contributed in any way to this effort, I express my gratitude. To the best of my ability I give credit to those who have helped. If I have overlooked you, please forgive me. My intentions were good.

FOREWORD

For most of us, when we were born, our parents were delighted and treated us as if we were the future kings or queens of the world. We were provided with good medical care, lots of love, and we were showered with much attention and affection by many people. Yes, most of us got off to a good start. Along the way, however, too many people are forced into "boxes," and they feel compelled to stay there.

Boxes come in all sizes, shapes, and colors. There are as many boxes as there are opinions. This book is designed to help you adapt to whatever box you've been temporarily assigned—and then to move you out of that box. It's difficult to say without sounding like I'm bragging, but this book covers an awful lot of subjects—everything from attitude, love, inspiration, relationships, goal setting, and motivation all the way to humor, encouragement, discipline, and a little bit of everything else. The messages are designed to encourage, build hope, and provide lively conversations at staff meetings and around the dinner table. They are structured so you will know more about living life, getting along with others, and charting your own course. Mostly this book is about persuading you that if others can accomplish the objectives they've accomplished and overcome the obstacles they've overcome, you also can do more with your life.

You will not find a single story in this book that says life is easy—because it is not. Life involves commitment, responsibility, dedication, persistence, and hard work. Since I've delivered many of these messages in seminars around the country and have written about them in newspaper columns, I can tell you that the principles are absolutely valid and will work, provided you take them seriously and apply them. If you do, I believe the messages will enable you to live a fuller, happier, more productive, more joyful, and better balanced life. That's a strong claim, but it's one I believe is true because the principles contained in these messages have helped many people to do exactly that.

I believe these messages will help you move out of any self-imposed boxes you may have built on your own, and especially those boxes that other people have placed you in. Another benefit you will receive is that you will be more excited about our country, your family, and your future. From that will come an enlightened lift in your attitude and enjoyment of life.

1

ATTITUDOSIS

"Let joy, temperance and repose
Slam the door on the doctor's nose."
—Longfellow

You can safely say that the right mental attitude is extremely important in virtually everything you do in life. This is especially true if you're going to build winning relationships in the home or on the job. People enjoy being around those who are cheerful or optimistic and generally excited about life. Few of us enjoy being around "prophets of doom." With that in mind, let me share some definitions that businessman Jim Norman passed on to me some years ago. If you can take a lighter look at life the way Jim does, you will brighten up the faces of the people you associate with.

Boredom—self-pity in disguise.

Change/growth—the process by which my inside begins to match my outside.

Compulsion—an overwhelming desire to destroy myself in the name of pleasure.

Denial—the ability to suppress the truth long enough to get what I want.

Envy—emotion produced by a belief that another's good fortune somehow detracts from my own superiority.

Fear—the need to run from the things I screwed up yesterday that I know will ruin my life tomorrow which I refuse to deal with today.

Honesty—a thing I have no problem with until I get honest about it.

Humility—being honestly and sincerely willing to learn a few simple things from other people, having no desire to strangle them in the process.

Love—when listening to you is more fun than thinking about me.

Low self-esteem—a modern psychological term that used to be called "shame."

Persecuted—the way I feel when I get what I deserve.

Powerless—a human being without faith in God.

Problems—God's method of revealing himself to anyone who is interested.

Rationalization—the process of convincing myself I need everything I want.

Self-pity—the door of depression, the fuel of fear, the anvil of anger, and the root of resentment.

Willingness—when I expose myself to the truth and refrain from shuffling the facts.

Sometimes taking an honest look at yourself really will put you out on the floor with foot-stomping, tear-rolling laughter. But I suspect that many of you saw your neighbor, sister, brother, mother, boss, etc. in the definitions above. That in itself is very revealing. The sad truth is that most folks have a pretty good self-defense system in place and don't want anyone to discover it, much less point it out.

> "A sunny disposition is the very soul of success, enabling a man to do double the labor that he could without it, and to do half the physical and mental exhaustion."
> —William Mathews

For instance, I'm sure many of you noticed that Jim's definition of self-pity was far from funny, especially if you related strongly to it. If you know someone who lives with the attitude of self-pity, you know how hard you work to avoid spending time with him or her. Self-pity is simply a symptom of attitudosis—a condition brought on by your neglect of others and their needs and by your extreme focus on and excessive attention to the most minuscule aches, pains, and inconveniences in your life.

You need to consider your attitude as seriously as you would consider the largest monetary purchase of your life. Your attitude helps shape your minutes, your day, your week—your entire life. It affects the way you feel, the way you look, even the way you respond to circumstances beyond your control.

Attitudosis cannot survive a strong, steady dose of uplifting literature or a regular donation of your time to a good cause. Make eye contact with someone who doesn't expect it and then give her your best smile. When you are willing to improve your attitude and you take action to do so, you'll enjoy life even more.

Message!

This is a reality check. I encourage you to read these first few pages again and reflect on them seriously.

———— 2 ————

WHEN THE MOTIVE IS LOVE

When our oldest daughter was a teenager, she came home from school one afternoon, hopped out of the car, and ran into the house, considerably excited, while her friends waited expectantly in the car. She rushed up to me and said, "Daddy, can I go to (such and such a place) with my friends?"

"There are two ways of spreading light: to be the candle or the mirror that reflects it."
—Edith Wharton

I responded, "No, Doll, you cannot."

She was somewhat stunned and said, "Why not?"

I responded, "Because I happen to know those kids are the wrong crowd, and they are headed to the wrong place."

She gave the typical teenager response, "Everybody else is doing it!"

I said to her, "Now, Doll, you know that has no bearing on whether you can do it or not."

Again she said, "Well, why can't I go?"

And again I responded, "It's the wrong place with the wrong crowd."

She persisted, and I patiently said to her, "Sweetheart, let me tell you something. Those kids waiting out in the car for you say they're your friends. Tomorrow or next week they might not be speaking to you. I just want you to know that there is never going to be anything that you can do, regardless of what it is, that will keep me or your mother from loving you."

I went on to explain that I loved her too much to permit her to jeopardize her reputation or possibly even her life. She stood, lips quivering, for a moment, then literally jumped forward, grabbed me, gave me a big hug and kiss, and said, "Thank you, Daddy! I really didn't want to go anyhow."

I have no idea what she told her friends, but the important thing is that she was able to blame me and save face with the kids in the car.

My wife, the Redhead, and I have had the experience of different ones of our children saying loudly on the phone, "Let me ask my parents," and then as they held the phone high in the air to catch our response they signaled us wildly to say no to their request. We have no idea how many times they wanted us to say no because they didn't want to be put in bad circumstances or how many times they just didn't want to do what was being asked. But we do know that sometimes children need help in saying no.

When you give directives to a child, especially a teenager, you must consider the nature of your child. All four of our children responded differently to the word *no*. Julie, our youngest daughter, would easily—even happily—accept our decision of "no" and then go about finding a way to do what we had instructed her not to do. When caught in the act of defiance, however, Julie always responded well to discipline. Once she had paid her price for disobedience, she did not repeat the offense.

> *"Politics is the science of how who gets what, when and why."*
> **—Sidney Hillman**

Our middle daughter, Cindy, always responded to no with anger—stomping down the hall, muttering under her breath and closing her bedroom door just a little too loudly. She might not speak to anyone in the family for two days. Cindy could hold out longer than the rest when it came to showing her displeasure. Her behavior was never as hurtful to us as allowing her to do what we didn't think she should do because of what might have happened to her.

I'm convinced that what kids need today are parents—not buddies. They need someone who will exercise mature judgment. Kids instinctively know—although they will argue to the contrary—that they really are not mature enough to make good decisions on some important issues. Like I say—they don't want a buddy at home. They want a mom and dad who love them enough to say no when no really is the best answer for the child. Yes, when the motive is love, even if the child doesn't fully understand, your decision will eventually be accepted.

Message!

Be there for your kids. Later, when you need them, they'll be there for you.

3

A MOMENT OF INSPIRATION

Sometimes one event, enthusiastically described, can have a dramatic impact on a person's entire life. In 1951 Bobby Thompson hit a home run that literally was the "miracle of the year." The New York Giants and the Brooklyn Dodgers were engaged in a struggle to win the National League pennant, and it rested on the outcome of the final game. The Dodgers were well ahead when the Giants started their "miracle run" in the last half of the ninth inning. Bobby Thompson stepped up to the plate and hit the historic home run that just barely cleared the fence to give the Giants the win—and the pennant. That moment was truly exciting.

"Children have never been very good at listening to their elders, but they've never failed to imitate them."
—James Baldwin

A young lad in Mobile, Alabama, was listening to the game on the radio when it happened. The announcer went berserk—literally. He lost control, screaming into the microphone, "It's a home run! The Giants win the pennant! The Giants win the pennant! It's the shot that was 'heard around the world.' " As the young lad listened, Hank Aaron thought to himself, *One day I'm going to hit a shot that will be heard around the world.* On April 14, 1974, Hank Aaron hit the home run that broke Babe Ruth's all-time record.

I would not want to leave the impression that the excitement from Thompson's home run was the reason Hank Aaron was able to break Ruth's all-time home run record. Aaron was a very talented young player who was supported and encouraged by his parents. Things were very tight financially in his family. Hank's father would leave a quarter for him so he could have lunch. He knew his father's quarter enabled him to maintain the physical strength and stamina he needed, but he also knew his father was giving up his own lunch.

Success of the magnitude achieved by Hank Aaron comes as a result of more than one person's effort. His parents obviously had a hand; his coaches certainly were instrumental in teaching him not only the fundamentals of the game but also the finer points of the game. However, it was Aaron's own commitment, drive, determination, and tireless efforts to reach his dream that produced the astonishing results.

I will always wonder if Aaron would have broken the record had he not been listening to that radio broadcast. I do know with certainty, however, that his decision that day to "hit a shot that would be heard around the world" caused him to approach his baseball goal with an expectation for the opportunity written about by Lilian Whiting: "To hold one's self in readiness for opportunity, to keep the serene, confident, hopeful, and joyful energy of mind, is to magnetize it, and draw privileges and power toward one.

> *"The highest point of achievement of yesterday is the starting point of today."*
> **—Motto of Paulist Fathers**

The concern is not whether opportunity will present itself, but as to whether we will be ready for the opportunity. It comes not to doubt and denial and disbelief. It comes to sunny expectation, eager purpose, and to noble and generous aspiration."

It is my conviction that the right words spoken at the right time can make a dramatic difference in a person's life. Fortunately, you can choose to be at the right place to hear those right words. Winners associate with winners. If you start out in life with the idea of seeking out and associating with winners on a deliberate basis, then your chances of winning go up. The wisest man who ever lived stated, "If we associate with the wise we will become wise; if we associate with the foolish we will become foolish." Much truth is contained in those words. Expose yourself to situations where you are likely to hear exciting, inspiring, potentially life-changing words. Be wise, and spend time with people who are interested in creating their opportunities.

Message!

When you choose the company you keep, you choose the messages of life you will hear, which means you choose your future.

4

REENTRY

All is not lost when someone ends up behind bars—especially if he is incarcerated in a North Carolina facility where Prison Fellowship teaches a course called Reentry Life Plan. "Reentry" teaches the benefits of a character foundation, a strong work ethic, relationship skills, goal setting, a winning attitude, etc.

> "Let a man have but an aim, a purpose, and opportunities to attain his end shall start forth like buds at the kiss of spring."
> —John Lancaster Spalding

Results: The recidivism rate in North Carolina is slightly over 40 percent, but in the facilities where the Reentry Life Plan is taught the recidivism rate is 6 percent. Everyone wins with this approach. Incidentally, in most cases the men and women involved were "habilitated"—not rehabilitated. They had never been taught the qualities necessary for success, so they bought into "the world owes me a living" mentality and ended up behind bars.

Question: Suppose the alcoholics, drug addicts, and lawbreakers don't want to be "habilitated" or to cooperate and be motivated? Answer: Actually, most of them, despite what they say, know that drug or alcohol addiction and anti-social behavior (crime and violence) are roads to disaster.

According to drug authority and brain chemistry expert Forest Tennant, M.D., some drug rehabilitation programs work even if the person doesn't believe in them. The addict often doesn't want to participate and resists going for treatment because he "doesn't have a problem" (denial) or he "can handle it." Many drug addicts/criminals have to be forced by law or strong parents to go into treatment.

However, one reason even "forced" treatment works is because the addict or lawbreaker knows that the person or law requiring him to take the treatment is concerned about him. Everyone wants to be loved and appreciated, and while they might protest or rebel, deep down they're saying, "I'm glad my parents love me enough to force me to do what is best for me."

The physical action of being in treatment, hearing things that make sense, and watching the progress of others who are in the program, motivates individuals to recognize their own problem and gives them the hope that they can be helped. The treatment centers have properly identified the drug addicts' "hot buttons." When addicts physically see the benefits of being drug-free, they recognize that progress in that direction would be in their best interests. Each bit of progress brings additional hope, and the hope breeds more action.

Point: Outside influence in the form of a forced physical action brings benefits which "motivate" addicts to continue treatment so their benefits will continue. Once the problem is solved and rehabilitation is complete, the abuser should maintain a healthy "fear" and understanding of the power of addiction. The motivation now should be to develop a game plan for staying drug-free and maintaining behavior that will keep them out of prison when they are released.

"Remember that every man at times stumbles and must be helped up: if he's down, you cannot carry him. The only way in which any man can be helped permanently is to help himself."
—Theodore Roosevelt

Actually, the steps are few and simple, but not easy. First, they must recognize that they are better off drug-free, and they must commit to staying drug-free. Second, they must take steps to make certain they don't fall back into the trap of addiction. Third, they must avoid any association with the former "friends" or associates who were part of the drug/law-breaking society and have nothing to do with them—no personal, phone, mail, or computer contact. This will be difficult because they might labor under the illusion that they are their "friends." Wrong. The Bible says, "Do not be deceived: 'Bad company corrupts good morals'" (1 Cor. 15:33 NASB). Fourth, establish a set routine. Go to bed, get up, and eat all meals on a schedule. Fifth, exercise regularly and join an organization that teaches ethical, moral values, like the church.

Message!

Love—real love—is doing for a person what needs to be done—not necessarily what the person wants done.

— 5 —
THE BEST NEWS

There are many different attitudes. Roberto de Vincenzo, a golfer from Argentina, beautifully displayed one of the best ones many years ago when he won the Masters golf tournament but was denied

Someone once said when you retire you go from "Who's Who" to "Who's That?"

the coveted green jacket. I say he won it because he had the lowest score at the end of four days. But his playing partner who kept the score had inadvertently written that he had made a five on one of the holes when in reality he had made a four. De Vincenzo signed the card, and when an incorrect card is signed, the player is disqualified. He had not cheated, but the rules stood. What was his reaction when he learned he was disqualified? Did he blame his playing partner? No, he said he made a stupid mistake. He accepted full responsibility himself. Now what kind of man is he?

Some time later he won another tournament. After they gave him the check, he spent a great deal of time in the

dressing room. He was in no particular hurry. When he got out to the parking lot, it was empty except for a young woman. She approached him saying she didn't have a job, her sick baby was at the point of death, and she didn't have the money to pay the hospital or the doctors. De Vincenzo signed his tournament winnings over to the young woman and went on his way.

The next week he was in a country club. One of the PGA officials told him he had been the victim of a fraud—that the young woman didn't have a baby and was not even married. De Vincenzo said, "You mean there is not a sick baby at all?" The official said, "That's right." De Vincenzo said, "You have just given me the best news I've heard all year long."

Where's your heart? What's your attitude? How would you have felt under those circumstances? Who had the greater problem—the golfer or the young woman? I think it is obvious, isn't it? How many of you think de Vincenzo really brooded the rest of his life over that woman who had beaten him out of that check? I don't think he gave it another thought. He was truly glad that there had not been an ill child. Now that takes compassion, it takes heart, but it also takes wisdom.

When is maturity in attitude reached? Is attitude a head thing, a heart thing, or both? Maturity in attitude is reached when you fully understand what you can change and what you can't change, and you respond accordingly. De Vincenzo couldn't change the figures on his score card or retrieve the

money he had signed over to the lying woman. Fussing and fuming would not change the reality of either mistake. He chose to *accept* what had happened and move forward. By doing so he saved his partner any further embarrassment and grief over the mistake. He showed everyone who witnessed the other incident his true character and was not made to look like a naive fool by an official who was all too proud to have the scoop.

> "Intelligence is quickness to apprehend as distinct from ability, which is capacity to act wisely on the thing apprehended."
> —**Alfred North Whitehead**

People with a good heart are exposed most readily in times of stress and ill fortune. De Vincenzo was more interested in the needs of his golfing partner and the welfare of a baby than he was in claiming to have been wronged. A heart like his, one that is honest, expects the best and holds no malice. It is developed over a lifetime. Roberto de Vincenzo at some point decided he was responsible for his circumstances in life, that he had control over how he responded to disappointment, and that a good attitude and a trusting heart offered many more rewards than their counterparts. Make the same decisions for yourself and relax into a more fulfilling life.

Message!

It's not what happens to you; it's how you handle it that will determine whether you are happy or miserable.

--- *6* ---

ASKING FOR TROUBLE—OR ASKING FOR BUSINESS?

For many years I've been a fan and friend of "Cadillac Jack" Hendrix of Little Rock, Arkansas. He sells Cadillacs—lots of them—and most of his business is from repeat customers. His circular to potential customers says it well. It begins with a question and follows with a list: "Do you know a car salesman who will—

- Take you to the airport and have your car serviced while you are away?

- Have your car picked up at your home or business for service?

- Have a loaner car supplied to you when your car is in for warranty work?
- Provide a mobile phone or beeper when your car is in for service?
- Have your car towed even when you get stuck or have an accident?
- Bring keys to you if you get locked out or lose your keys?
- Bring you up to five gallons of fuel if you run out?
- Jump-start your battery for any reason?
- Come out and change your tire if it goes flat?
- Help you plan a trip and reimburse you for expenses for hotels, meals, and rental cars if your trip is interrupted for warranty failure and your car has to be put in the shop for repair?
- Have your car washed when it is in for service?
- Have your car tags renewed?"

Cadillac Jack closes the questionnaire by saying, "As your personal transportation specialist, you will be able to call me by cellular phone or at my home any time. I will personally see that you get these services. If you find this information exciting, it is important that you ask for me because I am the only one who does it ALL!"

Sounds like he's bragging—or making a lot of wild promises, but his reputation for following through is firmly established. With his Christmas cards he also sends along a little mistletoe. When he delivers a Cadillac, he always takes a beautiful rose to the new owner. Jack has no idea what his commission is on any sale until he gets his check. He regularly sends news items to his clients that give them information they can use in their personal, family, and business lives.

"We tend to perform at about the same level as those people who are close to us."

—David Campbell, Ph.D.

That's why 80 percent of his business comes from 20 percent of his customers, which means that he sells cars to the same people year after year. It's safe to say that a good salesperson can sell a good car, but it takes a good person, with integrity and the right heart, to build a sales career.

And now for "the rest of the story." Cadillac Jack Hendrix, who credits his Sunday school teachers with having the greatest influence on his life, is more than just a superb salesman. Happily married for thirty-six years, the father of two children, and very active in his community, he's worked closely with Big Brothers and Big Sisters for many years. He has been heavily involved in the March of Dimes and served on the city board at Maumelle, which is across the river from Little Rock. He's also been president of an Optimist club, president of the Jaycee's, and at one point the youngest deacon in his church.

Jack demonstrates that you have to be the right kind of person and do the right thing to have all that life has to offer. Much to the surprise of some people, he proves that you can be the number one salesperson and a member of the highly prestigious Crest Club for fifteen consecutive years and still enjoy a balanced success in your home life, your spiritual life, and your community life. The concept that you can have everything in life you want if you will just help enough other people get what they want is at the heart of his philosophy.

Congratulations, Cadillac Jack, for being such an outstanding representative of the sales profession.

Message!

To receive all that life has to offer, you've got to be the right kind of person and do the right thing.

7

MISSING

"There is a great difference between worry and concern. A worried person sees a problem and a concerned person solves a problem."
—Harold Stephens

On a Saturday night, my wife and I returned from a fund-raiser and were greeted warmly by our Welsh Corgi dog and ignored by Timmy, the young cat with a long, fluffy tail we were keeping for Sunshine, our granddaughter.

The next morning when we returned from church, Timmy was missing, so we initiated a neighborhood search. On Monday morning I printed up a "Missing" bulletin and distributed it to all my neighbors. My daughter started calling the animal control centers, and we alerted the neighborhood patrol.

During this process, the thought occurred to me that all of us were busy, especially at our company since we were moving to a new location. Yet I was enthusiastically investing a substantial amount of time to find that little cat. That's

24

typical. Most people pull out all stops to recover a pet or a treasured relationship. We would "do anything" to change some things or to have them back.

Question: Doesn't it make sense to pay more attention to friends, relatives, and families whom you love? Are you really too busy to make the phone call, drop a note in the mail, get together for a meal, go for a quiet drive or a long walk, and invest a little time to show that love? Question: Why don't you just make the time?

I don't have a definitive answer, but I believe that in most cases it's more a question of procrastination than of deliberate neglect. We work at a frantic pace and come home to relax. Before we realize it, we've spent several hours relaxing in front of a television set that presents us with programs that make us no happier, healthier, nor give us greater peace of mind.

In addition, it's difficult to carry on meaningful conversations while watching television. Don't misunderstand; I believe some TV can be good and can offer company and comfort to shut-ins. But those things are not as important as spending time with those we love and cherish. Most of us plan to do exactly that "someday." But "Someday I'll" is a seductive mistress. Deep down we know that our actions this year will parallel our actions of last year and catch us falling back on the old saw of, "I'll call you later," or, "Why don't we get together for lunch?" etc.

Solution: Do it now. We have no idea what's going to happen tomorrow or even an hour from now in our own lives or in the lives of those we love. However, we do know that if we take action now to reinforce or mend some of our relationships, we'll look back with gratitude and say to ourselves, "You know, I'm really glad I took the time."

"You cannot cash checks on heaven's bank without first making the deposit of belief."
—Anonymous

I've never heard a busy person say, "If I had it to do over, I'd watch even more television, spend more time at the office, work even harder on my career." However, I've heard many people say after the loss of a loved one or the break of a relationship, "If I could do it over, I'd 'make' the time and handle our relationship differently." Think about it. Today, in many cases, you have a choice, but that might not be true tomorrow.

When Sunshine learned her cat was missing, she made the choice to invest her time searching for him herself. We thought it was a waste of time. But when she arrived at our home, she walked into the backyard and within three minutes shouted that she had found Timmy. He was stuck in the hedge, and apparently had been for some time. He was a mess!

Then, with considerable excitement, Sunshine told us she had asked God to protect her cat and let her find him.

That night she had dreamed that she would, and sure enough, there he was. Her faith is strong, and the God she worships is so great he is even interested in a young woman's cat. She made the time to pray for and seek what was important to her. If you do the same, your blessings will be many.

Message!

Spend time with those you love. One of these days you will either say, "I wish I had," or, "I'm glad I did."

—— 8 ——
THIS IS MOTIVATION

"Man is not the creature of circumstances. Circumstances are the creatures of men."
—Benjamin Disraeli

From the pages of *Crossroads*, written by Edgar T. Chrisemer and published in 1962 by Bruce Humphries of Boston, Massachusetts, comes this inspiring story:

Many years ago one of the large eagles in Scotland snatched from the front of a small cottage a sleeping baby wrapped in light clothing. Several people witnessed the event, and quickly the whole village turned out, trying to catch the eagle as it flew away with the baby. However, eagles fly and people don't, so the eagle landed on a lofty crag. Most of the people from the village lost all hope for the child's life. However, some of the villagers were determined to exhaust every possible avenue and make the effort to save the baby before conceding what appeared to be the inevitable.

First, a sailor who was between trips tried to climb to the high crag. But after a time he reached an impasse, accepted defeat, and abandoned the effort. He had failed, but others refused to quit. Next, a rugged, experienced high-lander who was accustomed to mountain climbing also tried. Although he got closer to the baby, he, too, could not quite make it, so he turned back in failure.

A frail peasant woman stood silently by while all of this was going on. Then she indicated that she was going to try. No one said anything, but it was obvious that everyone was think-ing if a healthy, young sailor and a rugged highlander had failed to scale the heights, what chance did this frail woman have? She removed her shoes and started putting her bare feet first on one shelf of the cliff, then another, and another until she rose to the level of the child. She lifted the baby from the eagle's nest while the villagers waiting below watched anxiously and fearfully.

The descent was even more difficult than the climb because one wrong step would now result in the death of two people. Carrying the infant added to the difficulty. But slowly, step-by-step, the woman descended the side of the mountain. Once she hit bottom the amazed villagers welcomed her. She was able to succeed while others failed because she had a dif-ferent kind of motivation. She was the mother of the child. Her love enabled her to scale heights the others could only dream about.

To say that this woman had a vested interest and a heart filled with love for the child would be an understatement, but those were motivating factors in her life. I'm confident the sailor and the highlander desperately wanted to save the child, but for the mother it was a question of the life of the baby she loved with all her heart. That's real motivation.

> *"Clear your mind of* can't.*"*
> **—Samuel Johnson**

Wouldn't it be wonderful if the love of *all* human life, not just our own family, would become a part of our society? I encourage you to remember that God loves all of us, and he has a vested interest in each of us. If that thought were to saturate our minds, wouldn't we be kinder and gentler to the people we deal with? Wouldn't we take more interest in the oppressed? Do you ever wonder just what we would be capable of doing and how much better our world would be if all of us showed genuine care and concern for other people?

Somebody has observed that there is so much bad in the best of us and so much good in the worst of us that all of us should be careful about what we say to and about the rest of us. To that we should add "and what we do for others." Who knows when a kind deed—or even a kind word—might have a substantial impact on the life of someone else?

Message!

Responsibility and commitment enable us to do things well.
Love empowers us to do them beautifully.

9

THE POVERTY MENTALITY

TV commercials, programs, articles, and a host of other things, in one form or another, make many of us want to "have it all." In too many instances, "all" includes the beautiful home as well as a place at the beach, in the mountains, or at the lake. To that list add luxury cars, exciting vacations, beautiful clothes, extensive trips, respect in the community, a wonderful family, and "everything" that a combination of several people might have in their lifetime.

"There is no calamity greater than lavish desires. There is no greater guilt than discontentment. And there is no greater disaster than greed."
—Lao-Tzu

The basic problem with this is that if we end up with "all"—meaning untold wealth and the things mentioned above—we still feel like we don't have "it all." And people who "want everything that everybody has" have a tendency to focus on what they do not have instead of what they do have. That's the "poverty mentality."

My friend and mentor, Fred Smith, says that over a period of time these people become greedy. They are like the old farmer who, when someone asked him if he wanted all of the land, said, "No, I just want the land that is next to mine."

The sad thing is that many of these people could have 90 percent of everything—meaning they have what 98 percent of the world would say is a wonderful lifestyle, and many things money will buy—but since they don't have a forty-foot boat and are only the _vice president_ of the company, their children are not super-achievers and their spouse is not a trophy wife or leader in the community, they feel cheated, and as a result they're not happy.

We seldom see greedy people who are happy. Happiness is not getting what you want but wanting what you have. This brings me to the major point of this section—gratitude for what we do have. The dictionary tells us that gratitude is an emotion of the heart; a sentiment of kindness or goodwill toward a benefactor; thankfulness. Gratitude is a virtue of the highest excellence as it implies a feeling and generous heart and a proper sense of duty.

It has been my observation over the years that you will seldom find a happy, ungrateful person. In most cases, ungrateful people expect others to do things for them to make them happy—and this simply is not the way life works.

Thomas Secker expressed it this way: "He enjoys much who is thankful for little. A grateful mind is both a great and a happy mind." Unfortunately, there are many people who do not have the capacity to express their gratitude properly. A. P. Gouthey put it this way: "Gratitude is the hardest of all emotions to express. There is no word capable of conveying all that one feels. Until we reach a world where thoughts can be adequately expressed in words, 'thank you' will have to do."

It has been said that gratitude is the sign of noble souls. John Miller really gives us a tremendous thought when he says, "How happy a person is depends upon the depth of his gratitude. You will notice at once that the unhappy person has little gratitude toward life, other people and God."

"There are two things to aim at in life: first, to get what you want; and, after that, to enjoy it. Only the wisest of mankind achieve the second."
—Logan Pearsall Smith

The message is clear: If we are thankful for what we do have, we will be happier and healthier. In addition, many of the other things either come our way or lose any significance for us. Hence, happiness is centered around all the wonderful things we do have.

Message!

Express gratitude for what you have. This increases the possibility that eventually you will have more to express gratitude for.

--- 10 ---

IS LANGUAGE MALE OR FEMALE?

Some disturbing information concerning profanity in the workplace from *Newsday*: The contention is that women today are using more foul language, particularly with other women, because they believe it gives them a "power position" and helps them move up the corporate hierarchy. According to the article, they have observed that men in power positions frequently use that language. I find that to be disturbing—and certainly misguided.

"God wove a web of loveliness, Of clouds and stars and birds, But made not anything at all So beautiful as words."
—Anna Hempstead Branch

Today you can walk down any street, attend social functions, or walk through many businesses—and you will hear language that no self-respecting person would utter a few years ago. Question: Is foul language helpful?

As a parent, have you ever taken your child out of a movie theater because of the sudden and unexpected use of foul language in the movie? Or did you walk out of the movie theater saying, "I sure am glad they used all of those curse words. It added so much to the movie"? Have you ever been seated near a table of diners who seemed to equate the number of curse words used with the degree of fun they were having? Did you leave the restaurant saying, "I really enjoyed sitting next to those raucous people. I never get to hear that kind of filthy language at home"? Vulgar language offends many people, and I believe it offends far more often than not. Why take that chance?

Foul language used by either sex is an indicator of immaturity and insecurity and a sure way to lose the respect of most people within earshot. In my opinion, a woman loses some of her femininity when she resorts to vulgar talk. If you happen to disagree with that, let me make a couple other observations.

Over the years I've been in many corporate offices with high-ranking executives. I've observed that the higher up in the hierarchy a person is, the more likely he is to be kind and gracious and treat his subordinates with respect and dignity. Eisenhower expressed it well when he said, "Leadership is the ability to persuade others to do what you want them to do because they want to do it."

Chances of getting results diminish if profanity is used in a demanding way. The subordinate might comply, but he or she will do it without any love or enthusiasm for the job. Conversely, if a person is respectfully asked in a voice that is authoritative, "We need this today because we have a deadline, and I'd appreciate it if you would get it done," not only will the job get done, but it will get done with care and respect.

> *"Conversation is the socializing instrument par excellence, and in its style one can see reflected the capacities of a race."*
> **—José Ortega y Gasset**

On the social side of the ledger, how many women marry men because they use foul language? How many men would be attracted to women who use language that is offensive to a high percentage of the population?

Research indicates that violence, especially in the home but also on the road and at least periodically in the marketplace, starts with filthy, violent language. All of us can remember occasions when someone brought up a subject and we said, "Don't get me started talking about that because the more I talk about it, the madder I get!" Anger, expressed in words, is frequently the first step toward violence.

Considering all of this, I hope the ladies will abandon their project of trying to be "like a man" by talking like one.

Ladies, you are far more effective and more persuasive when you are a strong, determined woman whose vocabulary is extensive enough that you can express yourself without the use of profane, violent language.

Message!

Your words can make you or break you. They are powerful. Charles Osgood was right: "Compared to the spoken word a picture is a pitiful thing indeed."

── *11* ──
GIVE PASSION
THE CREDIT

Any time you see a student with an average IQ perform great feats in the academic world, give passion the credit. When you see an athlete with only slightly above-average ability accomplish Herculean tasks, give passion the credit. Any time you see a parent successfully raise his or her children, despite physical and/or educational handi-caps and roadblocks that would stop an ordinary person in his tracks, give passion the credit.

"We may affirm absolutely that nothing great in the world has been accomplished without passion."
—Georg Wilhelm Friedrich Hegel

American independence was won because of the passion of our founding fathers. Every great religious revival has passion at its source. The civil rights movement was fueled by the passion of the civil rights leaders. The list is endless; passion plays a significant part in all great accomplishments.

The dictionary says that passion is "a strong emotion, an ardent love, zeal, eager desire, hope and joy." "Passion is the great mover and spring of the soul. When men's passions are strongest, they may have great and noble effects but they are then also apt to fall into the greatest miscarriages" (Spratt). All passions are good or bad, according to their objects. Where the object is good, there the greatest passion is too little. Where absolutely evil, there the least passion is too much. Where indifferent, there a little passion is enough.

Bulwer gives us some wise counsel when he says, "What a mistake to suppose that the passions are strongest in youth. The passions are not stronger, but the control over them is weaker. They are more easily excited; they are more violent and apparent, but they have less energy, less durability, less intense and concentrated power than in mature life." It's marvelous to understand the control of passions and direct them because when under control and with the right motive, passions can literally turn our world right side up and make it a better place to live.

In my book *Over the Top*, I stated that misdirected passion ultimately becomes an obsession. There is a substantial difference between having a "passion for something" and being "obsessed with something." Passion is positive, controllable, and tremendously energizing. An obsession is negative and disruptive. The person with a passion for what he or she does becomes a peak performer. Those who have an obsession with it become "workaholics." People with passion do what they're doing out of love for the people they're doing it for and for the results they expect to attain. The person with an obsession who becomes a workaholic will work out of fear and/or greed or denial.

Passion under those circumstances becomes negative. But on the other side of the coin, directed passion, mounted on an ethical/moral base, enables any person to utilize his or her full potential. The results can be awesome.

To be candid, I am a man of many passions. I have a passion to serve my God, my family, and my country. I have a passion to be and do the best I am capable of being and doing, regardless of what my mission of the moment happens to be. I have a conviction that passion, like courage, is transferable. When you work and associate with men and women of passion, that passion frequently is transferred to you. This is another reason we need to be careful about the people we associate with.

It is my conviction that when you are logically informed and emotionally inspired, you will be moved to recognize,

> *"To know of someone here and there whom we accord with who is living on with us, even in silence—this makes our earthly ball a peopled garden."*
> **—Johann Wolfgang von Goethe**

develop, and use all that is within you and become the best you can be. That's all God or man can ask of you. Fortunately, that will be more than enough to help you accomplish your worthwhile objectives. If you develop that passion, good things will happen in your life.

Message!

Commit yourself to a noble cause, and study carefully the possible societal benefits of that cause. Get busy in that cause, make it personal—and passion will grow. Then you can make a positive difference.

12

DREAMS ARE IMPORTANT

A number of years ago an experiment was conducted with a select group of college students. The students were hooked up to machines that could tell precisely when they went to sleep and when they started to dream. When the students started to dream, the clinicians would wake them up and then let them go back to sleep. Each time the students went back to sleep and started dreaming, they were awakened.

> *"It is only with the heart that one can see rightly, what is essential is invisible to the eye."*
> —**Antoine de Saint Exupéry**

After one night of this treatment, some of the students were nervous, fidgety, and ill at ease. After the second night, many of the students were irritable and cross, despite the fact that they had had a reasonable amount of sleep. At the end of just three nights of getting the same amount of sleep but with no dreaming, the researchers decided to end the experiment because some of the students were heading for some psychological difficulty.

Twenty-four hours later, most of the students were back to normal, and within a week all of them had returned to 100 percent normal. But the experiment proved something conclusively—that when you're asleep you must have dreams. I'd also like to emphasize that when you're wide awake, you also need to have your dreams. As a matter of fact, the only way you can keep your dreams from becoming nightmares is to awaken and go to work to make them a reality.

A dream held, visited, and revisited only in the mind causes people to feel much like the college students deprived of their sleeping dreams. They feel irritable and angry. They begin to head for psychological problems because they berate themselves for not pursuing their dreams. They develop an attitude of discontentment because they spend time thinking about how things "could" be if they would go after their dreams.

The basic problem is that many people are afraid of their own dreams. Perhaps their input has been negative. They've been told what they can't do instead of what they can do. Too many times they don't know what they want because they don't know what's available to them. As a result, many people get up and go to work today because that's what they did yesterday. Work is a habit. The job represents a necessary but unfulfilling paycheck; life becomes boring; and they drift from one mate, one job, one city to another. In short, they become "wandering generalities" instead of "meaningful specifics."

If you just realized that you have the basic problem outlined above, let me give you a couple of thoughts to consider: First, failure is an event—it's not a person. Yesterday really did end last night. Today is a brand new day, and it's yours. Second, understand that you can make radical changes in small steps. Remember, earthquakes and hurricanes get all the publicity, but termites do more damage than both of them combined—and the termite takes bites so small that you cannot see them with the naked eye. But they are persistent, they take lots of bites—and there are lots of termites.

"You have brains in your head.

You have feet in your shoes.

You can steer yourself any direction you choose.

You're on your own and you know what you know.

And you will be the guy who'll decide where you'll go.

Oh—the places you'll go."

—Dr. Seuss

President Calvin Coolidge said: "Nothing in the world can take the place of persistence. Talent will not. Nothing is more common than unsuccessful men with talent. Genius

45

will not. Unrewarded genius is almost a proverb. Education will not. The world is full of educated derelicts. Persistence, determination and hard work make the difference."

Make a decision to go after your dream. Get on a growth program, aim at a specific target, and persist until you reach that target.

Message!

Dreamers have had and will always have a huge impact on mankind—but only if in those wide-awake hours they work and use their creative imagination to make those dreams a reality.

13

DYSFUNCTIONAL FAMILY/DRUG ADDICT/ HIGH SCHOOL DROPOUT/SUCCESS

When you read the title, it sounds like one of those "too good to be true" stories, and in many ways it is. I'm talking about Rick Roosin, a man who had a limited formal education and very little business experience. He faced negatives and difficulties all his life. Nevertheless, he wanted to change. As he put it, "I knew for things to change I had to change. For things to get better, I had to get better." Truer words were never spoken.

"Adversity is sometimes hard upon a man; but for one man who can stand prosperity, there are a hundred that will stand adversity."
—Thomas Carlyle

Rick started going to Alcoholics Anonymous, where he learned one of the principles in which I believe so strongly— that you can have everything in life you want if you will just help other people get what they want. He learned that in order for him to stay sober, he had to work with others to help them stay sober. In AA (and I've had family members who've participated), as part of the program you are on call at midnight or even 3:00 in the morning when someone who is "off the sauce," but tempted to get back on, calls to get help from someone who had a similar problem but has successfully whipped that problem one day at a time.

Sober drunks sometimes stay up all night, encouraging and talking with their fellows who are struggling with a compulsion to drink. Person after person will testify that the only way they can stay sober is to help someone else stay sober.

This was Rick's first step to a better life. He said, "I developed some faith in the future and shut the door on my past." Great concept! For two years he drove an old 1967 Dodge Dart, rented a house, and then sublet several of the rooms to pay the rent each month. He started listening to motivational tapes and got interested in better health. He went from 200 pounds down to 163 and today is in the best physical shape of his life. He started reading the positive affirmations that came with his motivational tape series.

In the process of all of this, his belief system changed completely. He went from thinking he was not worth $500 a week to believing he was worth $25,000 a week. His income is now measured in the hundreds of thousands of dollars each year. He lives in a beautiful home worth over three-quarters of a million dollars, wears nice clothes, and has all the things that everyone says they want.

"Sorrows remembered sweeten present joy."
—Robert Pollok

But best of all, he sums it up by saying, "The important thing is I have a wife and two beautiful children, and I have more delight in my family than any other phase of my life. My family life is infinitely better than it was." He stated, "I wake up, I look forward to what I'm going to do that day. I love my life. I love the people around me."

Let me reiterate: He came from a many-generation dysfunctional family, from divorce, alcoholism, child abuse, etc. But he changed his direction in every area of his life— physically, mentally and spiritually. The results have been astonishing.

Here's the point. Failure is an event. It is not a person. If you don't like who you are and where you are, don't sweat it. You're not stuck there. You can grow. You can change. Just remember that you are what you are and where you are because of what's gone into your mind. You can change what you are and where you are by changing what goes into your mind. Psychologist Shad Helmstetter summed up much of what I'm saying with this statement: "You can't change from a negative mind-set to a positive mind-set without changing from negative talking to positive talking. To do that, you must change the input from negative to positive."

Message!

You can start from where you are and follow the steps of Rick Roosin. They will take you to where you want to be.

── 14 ──

PATIENCE HAS ITS REWARDS

My trusty 1828 Noah Webster dictionary tells me that patience is "the suffering of afflictions, pain, toil, calamity, provocation or other evil with a calm, unruffled temper; endurance without murmuring or fretful-

> *"Patience is the best remedy for every trouble."*
> **—Titus Maccius Plautus**

ness. Patience may spring from constitutional fortitude, from a kind of heroic pride, or from Christian submission to the Divine Will. Patience is the act or quality of waiting long for justice or expected good without discontent."

In today's world, Mark McCormack, probably the most successful sports agent in the business, has included among his clients Arnold Palmer, Jack Nicklaus, and a host of other famous names in the sports world. McCormack said, "In our twenty-odd years in business, 90 percent of our successes have involved in some way the need for patience, and

90 percent of our failures have been caused, in part, by lack of it."

Patience, or the lack of it, causes many people to blow up, lose friends and influence, and derail their own careers. People without patience are more inclined to take shortcuts, say what is necessary to achieve the immediate objective, or do what it takes to "get ahead," even at the expense of their integrity. The Center for Creative Leadership in Greensboro, North Carolina, studied forty-one executives, all of them successful people who were expected to continue their rise to the top. However, twenty-one of them derailed themselves while twenty did make it all the way to the top.

The study revealed that all of the executives had flaws. After all, none of us is perfect. However, the twenty-one who did not make it displayed such a consistency of repeated flaws that their shortage of integrity eventually undermined the trust others had in them, causing them to fail. It is true that if you can't trust an employee you won't promote him if you are "over him," or follow him if you are "under" him, if you have a choice in the matter.

To move to the top in the corporate world, or, for that matter, in our own private lives, we must have the trust, loyalty, and support of other people. In the Old Testament, the story of Job demonstrates both faith and patience, and to this day we hear people with a lot of patience described as having "the patience of Job." Patience is not passive; it is active. It is an indication of concentrated strength.

Benjamin Franklin, one of the wisest men who signed the Declaration of Independence, said, "He that can have patience can have what he will." Horace Bushnell said, "It is not necessary for all men to be great in action. The greatest and sublimest power is often simple patience."

> *"Genius is nothing but a greater aptitude for patience."*
> **—Georges-Louis Leclerc de Buffon**

Shakespeare observed, "How poor are they who have not patience? What wound did ever heal but by degrees?" Gil Hamilton said, "Patience does not mean indifference. We may work and trust and wait, but we ought not be idle or careless while waiting. Life has such hard conditions that every dear and precious gift, every rare virtue, every genial endowment—love, hope, joy, wit, sprightliness, benevolence—must sometimes be put into the crucible to distill the one elixir, patience."

The key to being patient is to be active. We don't sit around, twiddling our thumbs, and impatiently wait for things to come our way. We get busy working to make things happen. But we do so, though we might feel our time is past due. We do it without a chip on our shoulder—which is a good indication of some wood up above—or without anger or bitterness. We patiently work toward our objective because we understand that over a period of time the person who does the job and patiently perseveres in his or her efforts to accomplish greater things is the one who will be rewarded.

Message!

Patience and persistence built on a foundation of integrity and hard work are the surest way to long-term success.

———— *15* ————
MOTIVE IS THE ISSUE

Why we do things is extremely important. Do we act for personal gain, or are we working at filling a genuine need? Are we concerned about the other person, or is our motive purely selfish?

> *"The only gift is a portion of thyself."*
> —**Ralph Waldo Emerson**

I love the short story written many years ago by G. W. Target entitled "The Window." He tells of two seriously ill men who occupied the same hospital room. One was able to sit up for short periods to drain the fluid from his lungs, and his bed was next to the only window in the room. The other man had to spend all of his time flat on his back. Every day the patient by the window passed the time by describing to his roommate all the things he could see outside. The man in the other bed began to live for those periods when his world was broadened and enlivened by all the activity and color of the world outside.

The man by the window would describe the nearby park and lake, giving colorful descriptions of the swans and ducks. He told of children sailing model boats as their parents watched nearby. He would tell of the young men and women walking arm in arm among the beautiful trees and flowers. He gave daily weather reports in picturesque detail. In short, he described a glorious view of the world from his hospital bed. The man on the other side of the room would close his eyes and imagine the scenes his friend described, seeing in his mind's eye the pictures the man by the window painted with descriptive words.

One morning the nurse found the lifeless body of the man by the window. He had died peacefully in his sleep. As soon as it was appropriate, the other man asked if he could be moved next to the window. The nurse complied with his request and made the change. Once he was in place, he raised himself up on one elbow and looked out the window. But instead of the beautiful lake and all the wonderful scenery his roommate had described, he discovered the window was facing a blank wall. The man asked the nurse what could have compelled his deceased roommate to describe such wonderful things outside his window. The nurse responded that the man was blind and couldn't even see the wall. She said, "Perhaps he just wanted to encourage you."

Be grateful for what you have and not envious of what others have. After all, the other person just might be doing something nice for you.

The wisest man who ever lived also expressed it in a meaningful way: "A person's words can be life-giving water; Words of true wisdom are as refreshing as a bubbling brook" (Prov. 18:4 NLT). All of us can relate to that. We've met some people and spend a few minutes with them and felt encouraged and "better" as a result of the words they spoke.

> "One's eyes are what one is, one's mouth what one becomes."
> —**John Galsworthy**

Unfortunately, words can also be extraordinarily destructive. Many people carry the painful memories of cruel and condemning words from their childhood. If you use encouraging words, the recipient has a better chance of feeling better. If you use put-down words, these will drag people down.

When I was a youngster, my mother taught all twelve of her children that everybody could not be smart, but everybody could be polite and considerate of other people. To her good advice I would add that words are the primary way politeness and consideration are shown. Words are what we use most often to encourage other people in their daily lives. I'm convinced that when you use your abilities properly you can achieve success. I'm also convinced that when you help and encourage others to use their ability, you will have a better chance of achieving significance.

Message!

Words can build you up or tear you down. A little girl expressed this profound thought: "Sticks and stones may break my bones, but words can break my heart."

——— 16 ———
GO WITH THE FLOW

In our culture we frequently hear the phrase, "You need to go with the flow." While many times that's not good advice, there are those occasions when it certainly is.

> "I'll not listen to reason. . . . Reason always means what someone else has got to say."
> —**Elizabeth Cleghorn Gaskell**

In the late 1940s when Dwight Eisenhower was president of Columbia University, one of the problems he faced was that students ignored sidewalks and trampled the grass. Ignoring the many "Keep Off the Grass" signs, the students continued to take whatever route they found convenient as they hurried from one class to another. As a result, footpaths were worn along these routes. Many of the college officials wavered between anger, frustration, and genuine concern for the appearance of the campus.

Eisenhower did not get to be the allied commander in chief during the war, and later President of the United States, without his ability to see things from both sides. He came up with a simple, sensible, workable solution: He told them to forget the signs and fences and install sidewalks where footpaths had been worn. Then they removed the unused sidewalks and planted flowers and grass. It worked. He "went with the flow," and results were pleasing to the administrators and to the students.

I firmly believe you can have everything in life you want if you will just help enough people get what they want. Eisenhower helped the students get what they wanted, which was a fast, efficient route to their next class. Columbia University got what they wanted—a beautiful, neat, clean, well-organized campus.

Eisenhower's motive was good, but sometimes what appears to be a good motive turns out to be anything but that. Example: A motorist who was bogged down on a muddy road paid a passing farmer twenty dollars to pull his car out with his tractor. While he was grateful for the assist, which took only about five minutes, he felt the fee was a little high. With a degree of sarcasm in his voice, he said, "When you charge prices like that, I would think you would be pulling people out of the mud night and day." To this the farmer responded, "Well, I can't do it at night because that's when I haul water to that hole."

There is a certain amount of humor in this, but the odds are good that the motorist did not find much humor in the farmer's statement.

A gentleman needed a gardener, so he ran an ad in the paper. As a result, he received a letter about a man named Jones. The author of the letter said that Jones had an excellent knowledge of gardening and could make either vegetable or flower gardens bloom. He also described other admirable attributes of Jones. *That's just the man I need,* thought the man who was seeking a gardener. But he continued to read. When he turned to the next page, he read three sad words: "But he won't." Such is life, isn't it?

> *"Worry is double parking on the avenue of anxiety."*
> **—William Arthur Ward**

Since I am a speaker, I can relate to this story. As an after-dinner speaker, a man bit down on an olive seed and broke his dental plate. The fellow seated next to him said, "Perhaps I can help." He reached in his pocket and pulled out some dentures, but they were too large. A second set of dentures was too small. The third set was a perfect fit. The speaker, with much gratitude, said, "I thought I was really in trouble when I broke my teeth! How fortunate can you get, to be seated next to a dentist?"

His benefactor smiled and said, "I'm not a dentist. I'm an undertaker."

Just in case this has been "one of those days" for you, I hope these humorous little stories have added some enjoyment to it. All of us need to laugh on a regular basis.

Message!

Wisdom, laughter, common sense, and understanding the needs of others will build a dependable stairway to the top.

17

TO SPANK OR NOT TO SPANK

For years people with good intentions tried to convince parents that they should never discipline their children in a physical way that would inflict any discomfort on them. Everyone agrees that abusing a child is wrong and damaging. I was "switched" several times as a child, but each switching was the direct result of my refusal to obey

> *"For the very true beginning of her (wisdom) is the desire of discipline; and the care of discipline is love."*
> **—The Apocrypha**

the instructions my mother had carefully laid out for me. After each switching came the hugging. That's the procedure we used in raising our children.

Sometimes kids "ask for it." When my son was about eleven years old, he was having one of "those days". He was sullen, lackadaisical, and rebellious in his nature. Each incident of rebellion was an indication he was seeking discipline for his behavior. Finally, he crossed the line, and I pulled him over my knee and swatted him a couple of times with my belt, hard enough to be felt but not hard enough to leave any marks. Then I gave him a big hug and told him I loved him. Then both of us cried.

For the rest of the day I had a happy, loving, and obedient child. Children know instinctively when they are doing wrong, and they know that when they misbehave they suffer the consequences. Dr. James Dobson, the highly respected Christian psychologist, says that when a child deliberately is disobedient and rebellious, it results in an important contest the parents cannot afford to lose. This is where the authoritative approach is important. A child should never be punished for having an accident like spilling milk or dropping something on the floor. But children should be disciplined, including spanking, when they are rebellious. Otherwise, there will be serious problems later.

It's important to understand that we discipline a child for his or her own good. You punish someone out of your anger or loss of control. Discipline is good; punishment is bad.

Newspaper columnist William Mattox Jr. says the evidence is considerable that when biblical admonitions are followed, the results of corporal punishment are positive. "Using the example of a decade-long study of families with young children published in 1996, Diana Baumrind of the University of California-Berkeley found that parents using a balanced disciplinary style of positive reinforcement and firm control (including spanking) experienced better results than those who used highly authoritarian or highly permissive disciplinary approaches. Similarly, a 1995 government report from Sweden found that child abuse and teen violence actually increased dramatically after spanking was outlawed in that country.

"In a dark time, the eye begins to see."
—Theodore Roethke

"And in a fascinating new study just published in the academic journal, _American Sociological Review_, Brad Wilcox of Princeton University found that parents with orthodox religious beliefs are 'characterized both by strict discipline and an unusually warm and expressive style of parent-child interaction.' According to Wilcox, these parents employ a 'neotraditional parenting style that spares neither the rod nor the hug.'"

Mattox then says that it is important to note that no one is suggesting that parents should be quick to use spanking or that corporal punishment is warranted in every situation requiring discipline.

"Spanking should be used mainly as a backup to correct deliberate and persistent problem behavior that is not remedied with milder measures," advises Den Trumbull, a pediatrician who served on a special task force of the American Association of Pediatrics which reviewed spanking research. "It is most effective with toddlers and preschoolers (when reasoning is less effective) and should not be administered impulsively or when a parent is out of control."

"Ironically, one of the groups least apt to question the benefits of spanking are children whose parents have used spanking responsibly. According to a 1996 survey of 1,000 Americans conducted by the Voter/Consumer Research firm, more than four out of five people who were spanked as children report that it was an 'effective' form of discipline," says Mattox.

Message!

Discipline is something you do for the child—punishment is something you do to a child.

—— *18* ——

PRIDE AND
TEAMWORK

Briceville Elementary School has only 140 students in grades K–5, but in just seven years they have established a national reputation. An article by Morgan Simmons in the Knoxville, Tennessee, *News-Sentinel*

"Nothing is so firmly believed as what we least know."
—**Michel Eyquem de Montaigne**

identified the school as one of the eighty-eight schools nationwide honored as national Title One Distinguished Schools. Title One director Sally Jackson says they won the award because "the students have exceeded academic achievement goals for the past three years."

Academic achievements are impressive, but the impact on their own town and neighboring towns as well is even more exciting. The school is located three and one-half miles southwest of Lake City on state highway 116 in the heart of Tennessee's coal country. Yes, that's the part of America commonly known as Appalachia, and schools located here are not expected to do what this community, school, parents, teachers, and officials have accomplished. The reading scores have increased 31 percent over the past four years, and the math competency of the students has soared by 58 percent in the last five years alone. Ms. Jackson credits the combination of family, community involvement, the leadership of the principal, and a dedicated, qualified staff for the dramatic results.

For many years, with the decline of coal-mining operations, the population of Appalachia was declining, and the economy was in dire straits. In the fall of 1992, school officials and Title One staff members embarked on a series of overhauls that turned the school into a model for others to follow and also established it as the town's community center. The leadership of the town got together with all parties involved and for two days hashed out the new goals for the school. They identified the benefits, then the barriers, and designed programs to overcome those barriers. They took a "tough love" approach and hired the best teachers to go with the current staff. Those who could not meet the new standards were not around very long.

Even more important, they began an aggressive campaign to get everyone involved in the educational process, especially the parents. They held open house, but very few parents attended. They sent notes home to the parents—and that didn't work. Then they took the most effective step of all—the school staff began making phone calls and even personal visits. A parent advisory board was created to serve as liaison between the school, the parents, and the community.

In 1994, the Parent-Teacher Organization raised enough money to build a new playground. Today, that's the hub of community activity. Briceville students and the entire community use the picnic tables, swing sets, and running track. Sunday picnics are popular, and families gather together at the picnic tables. Much pride has been established, and each person does his or her share to keep all the litter picked up.

> *"Saying is one thing, and doing is another."*
> —**Michel Eyquem de Montaigne**

The gymnasium has become an after-hours community center for everything from aerobics classes and baton lessons to basketball games. A new air-conditioning system has been installed. With money from a technology grant, the school has built a multimillion-dollar media center next to the library. It's beautifully equipped with digital camera, scanners, computers, and a large-screen video monitor.

But the story doesn't end there. Preschoolers and parents from Briceville and surrounding coal towns such as Petros and Coalfield come to Briceville Elementary once a week for classes on learning development and health. The results have been spectacular. Walls have been torn down, and there is a sense of comradeship and teamwork with everyone in the surrounding area. Ken Phillips, one of the parent volunteers whose daughter, Lindsay, attends first grade at Briceville, says that the staff is excellent and they expect the students to learn. Most importantly, he says, "You can tell they care for and love them."

Briceville Elementary demonstrates what can be done when leaders bring parents, teachers, students, and community together. Here's a role model that every school and community in America can learn from.

Message!

Leadership, planning, and community involvement give life, hope, and meaning to the observation that "there are no hopeless situations, only people who lose hope in the face of their situation."

19

IT'S CALLED
"RESPONSIBILITY"

The fabulous best-seller *Customers for Life,* published by Doubleday and written by Carl Sewell and Paul B. Brown, offers some fascinating information. The authors contend that using inspectors to check out the quality of repair work done on cars by their technicians makes their technicians sloppy. They proved that when inspectors make the final check, the people who do the work are more inclined to get careless, knowing someone else will catch any mistakes they make. Inspectors also make mistakes, and experience proved that repairs and results declined when inspectors were added.

Sewell Automotive says their quality of work is now the best it's ever been because people feel more responsible for their

> *"I believe that every right implies a responsibility; every opportunity, an obligation; every possession, a duty."*
> —**John D. Rockefeller Jr.**

work and they like that responsibility. Their feeling and policy is that if a job has to be redone, the person who made the mistake must fix it, and he shouldn't be paid twice for the same job. That's only fair because comebacks hurt not only the customer who is inconvenienced but also the company itself. The Sewell people clearly understand that poor workmanship costs everyone involved. The reputation of the dealership is tarnished, and the company still has to pay for the heat, power, water, rent, and taxes while they're making the do-over repair for free.

The bottom line is the technicians are held accountable and, as a result, are more careful. The customers like the fact that they seldom have to return a car for a do-over. However, Mr. Sewell candidly admits that sometimes it's not the technician's fault. As an example, you can install a lightbulb, and it can work fine for twenty-four hours and then quit on its own. He says he worked as an inspector and passed many cars that were perfect when they left, but they came back because the repairs did not hold.

Obviously, no organization that sells the number of cars that the Sewell dealerships sell is going to turn every job out perfectly. But they learned long ago that the customer doesn't care what caused the problem or how many people approved the repair. If the work isn't done right, the customer will bring the car back.

The good news is instead of shrugging their shoulders and saying, "Mistakes will happen," they keep careful track of what work has to be redone, and "after we fix the job for the customer, we work to fix the flaw in our systems that allowed the problem to slip through." Mr. Sewell says that's important because "we found out a long time ago that if we just respond to problems, our quality suffers. Sure, we have to fix problems. But if that's all we do, we're going to keep having the same problems over and over again. It's far more efficient to find out what caused the problem in the first place. We do what's sometimes described as a 'root-cause analysis.' "

> "I hold that we cannot be said to be aware of our minds save under responsibility."
> **—Thornton Niven Wilder**

That approach will solve problems in the family, school, church, community, and even our nation. An example of the effectiveness of this approach is this: Sewell had a technician who did absolutely wonderful work with one exception. Every time he repaired a fuel injector, he'd never get it quite right. The investigation revealed that he never learned the proper way to do the repair. So they got busy and taught him how. Sewell quotes Deming, who says, "You can only know what you know." Since they identified the problem and took care of the training, the technician has been near perfect in handling those fuel injector problems. Now everyone's happy—the dealership, the technician, and most importantly, the customer.

When customers are consistently happy, they become loyal customers. That's why the Sewell dealerships are so successful. Their goal is to make everyone who comes through their doors a customer for life.

Message!

The customer might not always be right, but if you want to keep him as a customer you must make every effort to make things right with him.

—— 20 ——

THEY SAW IT ON TV

The July 1, 1999, issue of *The Dallas Morning News* carried the tragic story of a seven-year-old boy who killed his three-year-old brother by making a wrestling move on him that he had seen on television. Wrestlers use the move because they

"The direction in which education starts a man will determine his future life."

—Plato

are carefully trained and experienced in how to do it. In most cases, though their "victims" writhe in pain and are helpless before the aggressor for five or six falls, they suddenly recover and go on the attack.

Police Detective Dan Lesher, investigating the tragedy, said, "You've got to monitor what your kids see on TV. Parents are responsible for what their kids are seeing." Local authorities said they are not aware of any other deaths or serious injuries from wrestling-related moves, but the police and Dr. Jeffrey Bernard, Dallas County chief medical examiner, said they knew of a "handful" of similar deaths or serious injuries involving children in other states.

Several years ago an older boy in Oklahoma killed his younger brother by body-slamming him, not realizing the damage that could be done because on TV the guys always got up and continued the match. And now the Internet, which has over ten million sexually explicit porn sites, with a thousand new porn sites going online every day, is making serious contributions to the problem.

Solution

1. Parents must *take time* and get more involved with their children. For a child, love is spelled T – I – M – E. One of the best and simplest ways to spend time with your children is to make a family tradition of eating several meals together every week—especially the evening meal. When family meals are eaten together, the kids make better grades in school and are less prone to get involved in violence, drugs, sex, etc.

2. The input in our minds influences our outlook on life, and our outlook determines our output. The number of hours the typical eighteen-year-old has spent watching television, listening to music, and tuned in to MTV and video games is astronomical. Parents should restrict TV time and

watch the kids' favorite programs so they can discuss the issues with their children. Parents should remember that filth is filth and is objectionable, regardless of age.

3. Children should see their parents as role models they can copy. Parents should let their children see them reading books and magazines of value and then discussing appropriate articles with them. Today many books with short stories, filled with lessons and character values, are available. Reading those stories at the dinner table and discussing the issues is a marvelous way to teach life values.

> *"Youth is wholly experimental."*
> **—Robert Louis Stevenson**

4. Standards should be set. If something is illegal or immoral, it is not open for debate. If it is dangerous, the question for discussion should be possible gain versus possible loss. Example: One of our children wanted to get into sky-diving. We applied that yardstick with our daughter, and she decided not to get involved.

5. Violence today is demonstrated in road rage, when people become different creatures behind the wheel of an automobile and often violate the rights of others. The parent who uses a radar detector is sending an unmistakable message to the kids that if they are going to break the law, they should "be smart, kids, like your dad or mom. Show them you can outsmart the law!"

6. We need to insist that character education be installed in our school systems. It's ridiculous to contend that we can't teach kids the values of honesty, responsibility, dependability, hard work, integrity, and a host of other qualities that have nothing to do with religion, though they are taught by every major religion.

These are just a few things that can be done, but they will make a difference. If the right things are taught by parents and educators, chances diminish that violence and other antisocial behaviors will continue.

Message!

You are what you are and where you are because of what has gone into your mind. You can change what you are and where you are by changing what goes into your mind.

21

POSITIVE OR NEGATIVE?

As a general rule, America is divided into three groups: the positive, the negative, and the realists. It is my conviction that those who are optimistic and positive really are the realists.

> *"A great flame follows a little spark."*
> **—Dante Alighieri**

To begin with, my 1828 Noah Webster dictionary does not contain the word *pessimist,* although it does contain the word *optimist.* The pessimist and negativism are relative newcomers, created possibly by the super communications systems we have developed in the last 150 years. Much of the news featured in the media is of a negative nature. As a matter of fact, J. Allan Petersen, in his publication *Better Families,* says, "There is a pervading negativism that has infected and affected us all. Humanity is prone to a negative mental attitude."

Conversation is too often negative, critical, and gossipy. And it spreads like wildfire among friends and associates. This kind of negative talk is more destructive than we can imagine. It's still true that "one bad apple spoils the bunch." But the good news is that one upbeat, motivated, enthusiastic person who smiles and has a cheerful disposition can raise the sights and feelings of those around him or her.

I have made the observation that negative thinking, which I refer to as "stinkin' thinkin'," is more catching than the flu. One person who shares a negative observation in a group brings out the negative thoughts of everyone present. This can lead to a serious pity party. On the other hand, a positive comment from even one person can also light the fire of other positive thoughts. Before you know it, an optimistic group of people is talking in a positive vein. Since no one has ever proven that negative thinking produces better results than positive thinking, obviously positive thinking is the more desirable.

Dr. Petersen goes on to say, "Research shows that for every one negative thing you say to a child, you must say four positive things to keep the balance." And yet, too often we emphasize the flaws and failures. We are too slow to praise. That's sad because many people have commented that a sincere compliment restarts their batteries and keeps them running for days at a time. That's important because very few people will continue to work in a negative environment if they have other options.

In any economy, to have a productive person leave a job is very expensive. To replace the productive person you must advertise, interview many people, and go through the time and expense of testing and qualifying before a suitable replacement can be found. A positive environment, a simple "thank you for a job well done," an upbeat, friendly approach—all these are positive, friend-making processes that will reduce turnover and improve the bottom line.

> *"Gossip is mischievous, light and easy to raise, but grievous to bear and hard to get rid of. No gossip ever dies away entirely, if many people voice it: it too is a kind of divinity."*
> **—Hesiod**

We need to go back to the positive phrases that have lifted people out of the doldrums for years. This includes statements like, "If life hands you a lemon, make yourself lemonade" and "In every cloud there is a silver lining." Dr. William James, the father of psychology, says that the most important discovery of our time is that we can affect our lives by changing our attitudes. He points out that attitude is a choice; we can choose to look at things in a positive vein or choose to look at things in a negative vein. The more we take the negative approach and discuss our problems and the difficulties in society, the more problems we will have to discuss. It's amazing what the optimistic approach will do to improve our own personal lives, our family lives, and society in general.

Message!

The late Cavett Robert observed that three billion people go to bed hungry every night, but four billion people go to bed hungry for a word of encouragement and concern. Make certain it's not your son, daughter, husband, wife, or associate.

22

IT WAS A PRIVILEGE

Recently I was a member of a TV audience on a program that dealt with solving some of the problems in our society today. The open forum featured extraordinary football coaches D. W. Rutledge and Dennis Parker. A third participant was

former Dallas Police Chief Ben Click and the fourth was a former minister/educator, Rev. Russell White.

From the coaches we learned that they do not coach football—they coach boys and teach them how to play football. Coach Parker stated that he had never had a former player say to him, "Thank you, coach, for teaching me how to throw the football; it changed my life." But he's had many come back and say, "The story you told or the lesson you taught on a certain thing had a significant impact on my life, and I just wanted to say thank you."

Coach Rutledge emphasized that you've got to show the players that you're interested in them as persons, that you genuinely care about what they do with their lives and their education. The objective of both coaches is not just to win games but to make the young men successful in their lives.

When Coach Parker took over as head coach in Marshall, Texas, the football team had not won a playoff game since 1949. His first three years were rebuilding ones, and the team was 11–19. His last four years they were 45–3 and 14–1 in the playoffs, and they were state champions in 1990.

In 1984 Coach Rutledge took over a team that was the "doormat" in 5-A football. In 1988 they were state champions, and since 1990 they have been state champions three times and finished second three times. His overall record, including the slow start, is 184–23–5. Apparently, their system works.

Russ White was being recognized for his accomplishments in the Eagle Club from the state of New Jersey, where he did some extraordinary things working with youngsters in the inner city. He starts with them at age eleven, and by age fifteen they are flying airplanes with confidence. He points out that the first thing he does is require that they get a haircut that is businesslike and shows personal respect for self. He requires them to say "please," "thank you," "yes, sir," "no, sir," "yes, ma'am," and "no, ma'am." He puts his arms of love around them and makes it clear that he is interested in making them into adults, not rebellious kids. He believes with all his heart that he can take these underprivileged kids and make them into winners and champions.

"Only the educated are free."
—*Epictetus*

Chief Ben Click is a throwback to the old days of law enforcement. He's been a policeman for thirty-five years and has seen some disturbing changes take place in our society. He says we cannot pass enough laws or hire enough police to make an impact on the crime situation. We must work with parents and the community; we must teach our young people that we genuinely love them and that they must accept their responsibilities. He spoke with love and passion about his commitment to law enforcement, which really is a commitment to protect the rights of citizens and to give our youngsters a chance to grow up in safety and have successful lives.

One outstanding young man named Brandon spoke of what he learned in scouting and how it had been helpful to him. I shared that Judge Elvin Brown from Norman, Oklahoma, a twenty-year veteran of the judicial bench, said he had never had a juvenile in front of him who had spent a year or more in scouting.

One astute observation was about the farmer who, when told by a neighbor that he didn't have to work his boys so hard to raise crops, responded that he wasn't raising crops; he was raising boys. Yes, loving discipline, showing that you care, and giving hope were the underlying themes of the entire program.

Message!

Kids don't care how much you know until they know how much you care—about them.

— 23 —

LIFE IS LIKE
A BALLGAME

It has often been written that the world is
something like a baseball diamond with
home plate, a pitcher's mound, three bases,
and an outfield. The people in the game are
the players. When a player reaches first
base, it is generally through his own efforts

*"Knowin' all
about baseball
is just about as
profitable as
bein' a good
whittler."*
—Abe Martin

or through the error of a player who missed a fly ball, threw
too late to first, or simply threw the ball away.

The move to second base or the next level in life is a little
different. Sometimes we move to second by the efforts of our
parents and friends. Sometimes an advocate within our company who encourages us, trains us, recommends us, and
becomes our mentor and benefactor helps us to second base.

The same is true of third base. It could be a fly ball that
sends us to third, or a hit to right field. Again, we could get

there because the pitcher walked the two batters who followed us, or it could simply be because we carefully watched the pitcher's windup and the way the catcher handled the pitch and made a mad dash to third, "stealing" the base. At any rate, we're now placed in position to score.

The way to move on home most of the time depends on our alertness, speed, and the effort we are willing to expend. When the catcher lets a ball go past, or the batter hits a long fly ball to the outfield, in most cases it will bring us home. But effort on our part is always required. And the move from base to base gets tougher and tougher as we head for home plate. Here's why! When we get into scoring position, all attention by the players is directed at keeping us on third base. Both the infield and the outfield move in; relays are set up in case the batter hits a ball to the outfield. The catcher is alerted to be particularly careful to tag the runner. In short, the opposition gangs up on us.

Many of those things are also true in life. We generally get our first job through a personal recommendation or because we've had a solid academic career or developed a strong work ethic as we were growing up. But it takes a series of events and help from others, in most cases, for us to reach the top (home plate) in any profession. The physician has had great teachers along the way. The teachers themselves had teachers. The attorney had great legal professors who instructed and informed him about what to do. Along the way there was an individual who had a hand in building a character base upon which we could build a long-term success. It could have been through scouting, the church, or through the teachings of our parents and grandparents, particularly our mothers and fathers, each of whom taught us specific things not only by example but also by word and deed.

> *"The most decisive actions of our life . . . are most often unconsidered actions."*
>
> **—André Gide**

If the game of life is played fairly and to win, then when you head for home plate, you will not only have the privilege of scoring and being successful, but you will be greeted by your family, friends, associates, teachers, preachers—those who had a hand in making you who you are and what you are. Yes, it takes a lot of people to get to the top, and the more closely you work with those who help you, and the more mentors you have along the way, the more likely you are to accomplish your objective.

Play the game fairly and not only will you get to the top, but because you played by the rules to get there, you will have a long and pleasant stay. Not only that, but you'll have lots of friends to congratulate you on your success.

Message!

Individuals score points, but teams win games. This is true in athletic events and in life. If you make it in life, your "team" of parents, teachers, ministers, etc., will have played a major role in your success.

——— 24 ———

WHAT YOU COULD DO IF YOU DIDN'T KNOW YOU COULDN'T

Many years ago when I got involved in positive thinking, inspiration, and motivation, I read about a man who was pinned beneath the family car when the jack slipped. His wife, who was of average size and strength, lifted the car just enough for him to slide out from under it.

"We never do anything well 'til we cease to think about the manner of doing it."
—William Hazlitt

There was much speculation about how she was able to do that, because everyone doubted that she could lift the car again. Some say she was able to lift the car because she had no idea what she couldn't do and her subconscious mind "kicked in" and supplied the needed strength. Others say that love lifted the car because the life of her husband, the man she loved, was in jeopardy, enabling her to lift the car. There may be some who will contend it was because she was a math major and knew that she plus God equals enough, and with God's help she could lift the car.

Whatever the reason, she was able to do it. It makes us wonder about the many things we could do if we didn't know that we couldn't do them. Many people never make a serious effort to achieve worthwhile objectives because they assume they can't reach them.

Here's another story that demonstrates what even a little extra effort can produce. Sir Walter Raleigh attended a prestigious boarding school when he was a youngster. He was an excellent student and wanted to be number one in his class. However, one lad always finished ahead of him, so he determined to discover the secret. Each night when he prepared for bed, he looked across the grounds that separated his room from that of his competitor and noticed that his candle was still burning. One night he noticed that the other boy studied only about fifteen minutes longer than he did. After that, Sir Walter Raleigh studied an extra twenty minutes every night. At the end of the year he was the number one student.

I've often wondered how many students miss out on a college scholarship because they did not study an additional twenty minutes each day. Research shows that over

98 percent of all scholarships are either academic or hardship, so some deserving students miss out not because of lack of ability, but because of lack of effort. Many times people grow frustrated because promotions or raises don't come as fast as they think they should, so they jump ship when just around the corner the promotion awaits.

> *"Eternity was in that moment."*
> **—William Congreve**

In the field of athletics, we have all seen the tired athlete near the end of the game simply run out of gas and lose because he or she had not been expending the effort on a daily basis to get into top condition for the event. Yes, as Joe Frazier, the former heavyweight champion of the world, said, "You can cheat on your roadwork and nobody will know until you step into the ring, and then the bright lights will expose your lack of training to the world." It's true. A little extra effort separates the winners from the could-have-beens.

I have often used the phrase "and then some," pointing out to my audiences that you should keep every promise, *and then some;* give your clients or customers everything they expect, *and then some;* give whatever you do an honest effort, *and then some.* I first learned those words from former secretary of state James Byrnes, who used that phrase when someone asked him to explain his success in life and in the political arena. I believe that little extra effort—that going ahead from where they are to do the best they can with what they have, *and then some*—is what separates the successful from the would-be successful.

Message!

When you go the extra mile, you are seldom delayed by a traffic jam.

25

PARENTS MAKE THE DIFFERENCE

A recent study by the Center on Addiction and Substance Abuse (CASA) found that parents are the keys to keeping their kids off drugs. However, they point out that just having mom and dad around is not the solution within itself, but what mom and/or dad do is important. That importance is dramatically increased when both

"The greatest pleasure I know is to do a good action by stealth, and to have it found out by accident."
—*Charles Lamb*

mom and dad take time to build relationships with their teenagers. It begins with loving them unconditionally—not because they are handsome or beautiful, not because they are obedient, etc. Any time you put a condition on your love, you are raising a child who is insecure. Insecure kids typically seek the wrong company and get involved in destructive activities. It takes time to build relationships with your kids. They need to know that your conversational door is always open to them.

The survey showed that teens are far more likely to talk to mom than to dad. Fathers, take time to build relationships with your children. Less TV time and more talking and listening are critical. Eating together makes a huge difference. Even two or three meals a week together will substantially curtail drug use, sexual activity, and violent acts.

Incidentally, 71 percent of teens report they have an excellent or very good relationship with their mothers, while only 58 percent have that relationship with their fathers. Twice as many teens say it's easier to talk to mom than dad about drugs, and twice as many teens who have never used marijuana credit mom with that decision. Teens are three times more likely to rely solely on mom than on dad when they have important decisions to make. Dad needs to get more involved, but it's the two-parent families that have the best chance for keeping their kids off drugs.

Other research indicates that if we start the day with our children properly and end the day properly, the time in between will go better. Getting up just ten minutes earlier and slowly and lovingly awakening the children is infinitely better than the last-minute routines that involve fast (or no) breakfasts, short tempers, and the stress and anxiety that accompany a rushing household. Those extra minutes give the family a more leisurely breakfast and time to be kind and affectionate with one another. At bedtime you turn the TV off and listen to countless ridiculous questions, designed primarily to delay bedtime. After a few minutes of silliness the frivolous talk generally ends. That's when your child reveals what is on his or her heart and bonding takes place.

> *"No young man believes he shall ever die."*
> **—William Hazlitt**

Good news! Twenty-three percent of teens now say drugs are their biggest problem, down from 29 percent just a year ago and 35 percent two years ago. Kids who attend schools where drugs are available are at twice the risk of substance abuse as teens attending a drug-free school, nearly three times as likely to smoke cigarettes, three times more likely to have tried pot, and twice as likely to know a teen who uses cocaine or heroin.

Interestingly enough, 75 percent of students in Catholic and other religious schools say their school is drug-free, compared to 40 percent of public school students. Joseph Califano, former secretary of Health, Education, and Welfare, says, "Parent power is also key to drug-free schools. When parents feel as strongly about drug-infested schools as they feel about asbestos-infected schools, we'll have drug-free schools in America." I agree, but it still gets back to parents and their relationships with their kids. The example they set and whether or not they smoke and/or drink has a strong bearing on their kids' drug use. That's an awesome responsibility, but I'm confident that parents who are reading this would "do anything" to keep their kids out of the drug jungle.

Message!

Parents make the difference, and parents who set the example and talk and listen to their kids' interests and concerns make the biggest difference.

—— 26 ——
WHY KIDS KILL KIDS

FBI research indicates that all of the "kids who kill kids" have two things in common, whether in Pearl, Mississippi; Paducah, Kentucky; Jonesboro, Arkansas; or Littleton, Colorado.

"Blessings are on the head of the righteous, but violence covers the mouth of the wicked. The memory of the righteous is blessed, but the name of the wicked will rot."
—Proverbs 10:6–7

First, these kids seldom, if ever, went to church where they might have been subjected to the Ten Commandments or heard the message of "be ye kind, one to another," the Golden Rule, and other teachings that help develop law-abiding citizens.

Second, they frequently played interactive video games where they practiced "shooting" their victims, which were so lifelike they looked real. They bled, they screamed, they exhibited the pain of having been shot. The sense of "taking them down" was very real, so they were living out the fantasy in their own minds. In the process, they were desensitized and took little or no thought of the long-term consequences of their actions. They were in control and growing less sensitive to the value of human life until—for them—it had no value at all.

The killers were in many ways "misfits" and did not gain acceptance among their peer groups. Their only exposure to what the church teaches was the way believers are frequently depicted on television, in movies, and on the Internet. Power and violence are two dangerous and attractive lures for a troubled youngster who has been fed the power concept, combined with hatred and fear as well as anger.

Incredibly enough, one of the Columbine students had never shot a gun before. And yet, because of the virtual reality interactive videos, he had been carefully taught a very effective way to shoot. Each of his first eight shots was right on target, except this time they claimed living victims. An FBI agent with many years of experience told me that he doubted that even with his training and hours on the firing ranges he could have shot as well. In short, not only were the young killers desensitized, but they had also been trained to kill.

In a twelve-year study on bank robbery conducted by the FBI in Dallas, one thing was consistent with every robbery. Many had the two above factors (the robbers seldom, if ever, went to church, and had watched lots of violent video and TV), but the third factor was their fascination with violent pornography. In violent pornography the man is in control—he dominates, he's the boss, and he's the one who dictates to others. When bank robbers walked into banks with their guns, they were in control— "I am now the boss; you will do what I tell you. You will obey, or I will blow you away."

> "Nonviolence is the first article of my faith. It is also the last article of my creed."
> —Mahatma Gandhi

When a person has been saturated with violent input and is convinced that life is unfair and he feels rejected, he often turns to violent actions. Strangely enough, many people, led by the media, will deny that watching pornography or violent videos/TV has any impact on their behavior. Common sense dictates otherwise.

Action: Ban violent, interactive videos from your home. Know your children's friends and find out if those kinds of videos and games are being used in their homes when your child is present. It's true that you can't control everything, so you must set the right example from infancy. This idea of some things being "for adults only" is absurd. Filth, violence, and profanity benefit no one, regardless of age. The parents must set the example by not watching gratuitous sex and violence on TV and by explaining to their children in a loving way why they do not watch it. If kids have been taught this from early childhood, it won't even be an issue when they become teens. Be proactive and protect your children.

Message!

Your children pay more attention to what you do than what you say.

---- *27* ----

THE WEIGHT
ROLLER COASTER

When she was just five years old, Rosalie
Bradford felt the pain of abandonment and
found solace in food. She weighed 250
pounds when she met her husband. By the
time their son Rob was born, her weight
had escalated to 374 pounds. She chose to
be a stay-at-home mom and started eating
10,000 calories a day. She weighed 500

> *"The desire of
> knowledge, like
> the thirst of
> riches,
> increases ever
> with the
> acquisition of
> it."*
> **—Laurence
> Sterne**

pounds by the time Rob graduated from *nursery school.*

At that point she elected to stay in bed, and her weight
continued to escalate. In 1970 when she went into the hospital for an intestinal bypass, two beds had to be chained
together to accommodate her. Postoperative complications
resulted in a blood infection that turned her leg blue-green
and made her temperature rise to over 105 degrees. The leg

required twelve surgeries and caused her considerable pain and frustration.

Discharged from the hospital, Rosalie went home and "took an eight-year nap." She continued to gain weight; her husband had to quit his job and devote himself to her full-time care. At this stage in her life, she no longer just wanted food; she had become addicted to food. She was demanding, and she chastised her husband and anyone else if they refused to bring her food. Throughout the ordeal her husband prayed for her. But he never considered abandoning her because, he said, he felt that "when you got married, that you were married to that person until 'death do you part.'"

By 1988, Rosalie weighed twelve-hundred pounds and had an eight-foot girth. Bathing was an hour and a half ritual, and there appeared to be no hope. At this point a friend wrote to Richard Simmons about Rosalie. He sent her his diet plan and for the next eighteen months called her almost every day. It was some help; however, she still struggled with losing and gaining, losing and gaining again. Chances are good that many of you who read these words will have suffered from the same experience. For twenty-four years of my life I was on the weight loss/weight gain roller coaster.

Rosalie also invited a Christian psychologist to counsel her. The first thing he did was tell her to "fluff up her bed pillows and talk to Jesus." She decided to give control of her problem to God. She recognized she couldn't solve the problem, nor could any individual solve it for her. She quit thinking of goals in terms of the future and concentrated on today. Now she was ready to reenter the world.

The story does have a happy ending. After being a prisoner of fat for almost ten years, Rosalie Bradford walked out on the porch outside her bedroom and stayed as the warm day turned into a cool night. "I could see the stars," she said, "I could see the top of the trees and didn't have to look out a window." Just a few months ago Mrs. Bradford moved to Auburndale, Florida. She weighs 304 pounds and credits God with helping her recover. "God did for me what I couldn't do for myself. He made me aware of my responsibility. I'm responsible for what I eat."

> *"Live as you will have wished to have lived when you are dying."*
> **—Christian Furchtegott Gellert**

Yes, you can become addicted to food just as you can become addicted to tobacco, drugs, alcohol, pornography, etc. In many of these cases God is the only solution. Every successful drug rehab and alcohol-related program I'm familiar with ultimately recognizes that these are addiction problems that only God can solve. What a shame so many people use the Creator of the universe as a last resort instead of the first resort. Reversing that order would certainly bypass many difficulties people encounter along the way.

The good news is that Rosalie Bradford and many others finally came to the same conclusion. They need help, and they can receive help beyond what man can do.

Message!

With God's help you can change and take control of your life. You plus God equals enough.

── 28 ──
IT'S THE LAW

A fascinating new law has been passed in Louisiana requiring students from kindergarten through fifth grade to address their teachers as "Sir" or "Ma'am," or with the courtesy titles "Miss," "Mrs.," "Ms." or "Mr." Some of the teachers supported the measure as a tool for classroom discipline. Others opposed it as a waste of their limited teaching time. Lawmakers, assured by the government that it would please voters, overwhelmingly embraced it.

> *"He that will have his son have a respect for him and his orders, must himself have a great reverence for his son."*
> —**John Locke**

No one asked, but here is my opinion. I enthusiastically endorse the idea for practical "survival" reasons. The first act of violence at home is generally preceded by violent language. Dr. Jane Healey, in an article in *Bottom Line Personal*, said, "The development of human language is the development of human thought, and if kids don't talk and listen, they don't think effectively either. The person who teaches your child to talk teaches your child to think."

Unfortunately, respect for authority is a missing element in our society today. Gangs use lack of respect as an excuse for beating or even killing anyone who "disses" them. If respect for teachers, peers, and parents is taught in the classroom and if children are complimented and congratulated when they give a courteous, respectful answer, it will make for a friendlier environment and prepare them for the business world when they complete their formal education.

Louisiana used superb judgment in the way they implemented this new law. They started by teaching it from kindergarten through fifth grade. Next year it will apply to sixth graders and so on until it is taught and required in all grades. I'm convinced that one of the benefits will be improved grades. When courtesy and respect are shown in the classroom, there will be less talking and less disturbance, allowing the teacher more time to teach. It will take time for this to take effect, and some will rebel, but it's more than a cliché to say that behavior that's recognized and rewarded will be repeated. This is true whether the behavior is bad or good.

A pleasant compliment from the teacher when a child responds respectfully will take only a second. A "thank you, John/Sally, that's great," is all that's necessary. Most of us will watch with interest the results of this law. I believe other states will follow suit in a year or two. Too bad it has to be a law.

Now that we've dealt with courtesy and respect, let's look at the other side of the coin and list some of the results of using gutter, profane, or violent language:

> *"Shall we make a new rule of life for tonight: always to try to be a little kinder than is necessary?"*
> **—James Matthew Barrie**

1. It "honors" your parents and influences your children and grandchildren to continue your legacy.

2. It demonstrates your extensive vocabulary and displays your communication skills.

3. It proves you are versatile and flexible.

4. It enhances your career "opportunities."

5. It gives you experience in constantly finding new jobs.

6. It improves your chances of landing and keeping a good mate.

7. It enables you to "fit in" with like-minded people.

8. It impresses those who appreciate so-called "adult" language. (Filth is still filth, regardless of one's age.)

9. It clearly separates you from those who have "class."

10. It gives you extensive experience in seeking new friends.

11. It substantially reduces your sensitivity.

12. It dramatically increases your probability of committing violent acts.

13. It opens the door to numerous minimum wage jobs and friendship with like-minded associates.

14. It helps others to get to know you quickly and well because out of the heart the mouth speaks.

15. It enables you to move to lower levels more quickly.

16. It enables you to embarrass, antagonize, and irritate more people than almost any other single act.

Message!

Your words identify and define who you are, what you think, and ultimately where you will go. Adult language like "commitment," "responsibility," "integrity," "dedication," etc., replete with words like "good," "best," "fair," "hope" and "love" will greatly enhance your personal, family, and professional life.

—— 29 ——

THE SUCCESS FACTOR

From my perspective, long-term success is the only way you can really measure success. Occasionally, a heroic act by an individual may make him or her a professional success. For example, Colin Kelly sacrificed his life at the beginning of World War II to sink a Japanese war ship and save the lives of countless Americans. Colin Kelly's character made his sacrifice possible, and that's the kind of character you will always find in truly successful people.

> *"The secret of success is constancy to purpose."*
> **—Benjamin Disraeli**

Without character there is no trust. Successful people are men and women of integrity. They do the right thing, which means they are trusted and they have no guilt to deal with. With integrity they have nothing to fear because there is nothing to hide.

Another quality I attribute to people who are long-term successes is the quality of faith. There comes a time in every person's life—and in most cases it happens many times—when he or she encounters difficulties or problems for which there are no human answers. This is where faith in God is critically important. Faith in Jesus Christ has made a big difference in all facets of my life.

Other qualities that are important are pure, dogged persistence and overwhelming desire. According to *The Executive Speechwriter Newsletter* (vol. 12, no. 3), "Desire kept young W. Clement Stone on Chicago's street corners selling newspapers. Desire later made him one of the wealthiest people in America as principal owner of Combined Insurance Corporation of America.

"Desire made Jim Marshall one of the most indestructible players in professional football. Marshall started 282 consecutive games and played defensive end until he was forty-two. Teammate Fran Tarkenton once described Marshall as 'the most amazing athlete to play in any sport.'

"Desire energized John Havlicek, to earn the nickname 'Mr. Perpetual Motion.' As a player for the Boston Celtics, Havlicek gave 200 percent every game for 16 straight seasons. Hustle, leadership, and guts made Havlicek a player by which others were measured. People with desire work harder, are passionate about their goals, and are driven by an intense thirst to be better."

It is also essential to believe that what you are doing with your life makes a difference in the lives of others. Our mission statement is to be the difference-maker in the personal, family, professional, and spiritual lives of enough people to make a positive difference in the world. I recognize it is a presumptuous mission statement, but with the advent of modern technology, we can communicate in ways never dreamed of just a few years ago. I get a substantial amount of mail from people who tell me that our concepts have made a positive difference in their lives.

> *"If one advances confidently in the direction of his dreams, and endeavors to live the life which he has imagined, he will meet with a success unexpected in common hours."*
> **—Henry David Thoreau**

I hasten to add that if you are staying home full-time to raise your children, you are most definitely making a difference in the lives of others. The long-term success of our country depends on the difference you make in the lives of your children. An article in the October 1999 issue of *Readers Digest* states: "According to the U.S. Department of Education, two out of three high-schoolers won't make it to college if they belong to a single-parent household, have an older sibling who dropped out of high school, repeat a grade, change schools more than twice or have lower than average grades." The obvious solution to helping your children be all they can be is to offer them a secure home life with both parents present, pay close attention to how they are doing in school, and do what it takes to see that they always make the grades they need to make. In fact, everyone's potential for long-term success starts at home.

Message!

Our children are our only hope for the future, but we are their only hope for the present and their future.

THAT POSITIVE-THINKING STUFF

The January 9, 2000, issue of *The Dallas Morning News* carried a fascinating article about the effects of positive thinking and optimism. The newspaper reported that dozens of recent studies show that optimists do better than pessimists in work, school, and sports. They also suffer less depression, achieve more goals, respond better to stress, wage more effective battles against disease, and even live longer.

> *"It is our less conscious thoughts and our less conscious actions which mainly mold our lives and the lives of those who spring from us."*
>
> **—Samuel Butler**

Dr. Martin Seligman, a University of Pennsylvania psychologist, cited another scholar's spadework stating there were forty-six hundred papers in the psychology literature on depression, but only four hundred on joy over the last three decades. He believes much of that will change in the twenty-first century.

The questions are: What is this "positive thinking" stuff? How does it work? What are the benefits in addition to those mentioned above? I often use the analogy that you can walk into a dark room, flip a switch, and the room will instantly be lit. Now, obviously, flipping the switch did not light the room. What it did was release the electricity that had been generated earlier. If there were no electricity, the room would still be dark.

Students who take our positive-thinking, character-based course in school make better grades. That's not to say that positive thinking makes them smarter. What it does is release the information they have acquired from their books. All of us have heard students moan as they go in to take a test, "You know, I always think of my answers after I've left the classroom," or, "I never do good on tests. I know the stuff; I just can't remember it during a test." Those are the typical words of pessimists. On the other hand, the positive-thinking optimist who has prepared his lessons and studied adequately walks into the test room expressing confidence that he will be able to do well on the test. That positive thinking releases the information that he has carefully acquired over a period of time. His test scores are considerably better than his ill-prepared, and thus pessimistic, classmate.

The bottom line is that positive thinking releases the knowledge, experience, training, facts, educational acquirement, and background information that is stored in your mind. Positive thinking simply permits you to use the information and knowledge that you have acquired. I must add that positive thinking won't let you do anything, but it will let you do everything better than negative thinking will.

> *"Do not pray for easy lives. Pray to be stronger men! Do not pray for tasks equal to your powers. Pray for powers equal to your tasks."*
> **—Phillips Brooks**

One part of Dr. Seligman's research created a lot of excitement and enthusiasm when it revealed that optimists live a couple of years longer than negative people do. It got everyone's attention. Dr. Seligman pointed out that "one reason [positive people live longer] may be that optimists do a better job of staying out of harm's way." That's what a recent study drawing on records from a project begun eight decades ago indicated. The study revealed that pessimistic people appeared more prone to accidents and violence, including car wrecks, household mishaps, even homicide. Optimists confront troubles head-on and deal with them in a more realistic way, while "pessimism was associated with denial and a giving-up response," according to Dr. Charles Carver of the University of Miami.

Speaking from personal experience, I vividly remember when my career was on a downhill slide back in 1952 and

I was feeling rather negative when I picked up Dr. Norman Vincent Peale's *The Power of Positive Thinking*. It had a profound impact on my attitude and my life, and I immediately started getting positive results in my business. Yes, positive thinking really does work, and it should be embraced by everyone who wants to get more out of life.

Message!

Whether you think you can't or think you can, you are right.

——— 31 ———

KINDNESS AND COURTESY ARE IMPORTANT

There is a growing concern in the market-place that lack of consideration for our fellow workers, and just downright rudeness, are affecting team spirit and productivity. It seems that the pressures increase as our electronic efficiency increases. There is the feeling in a super-efficient organization

> *"Rude am I in my speech, And little bless'd with the soft phrase of peace."*
> **—William Shakespeare**

that to be more direct and action-oriented is the order of the day. Unfortunately, many people take that one step further and become rude and demanding. As a result, considerable discord in the company structure increases.

Christine Pearson, a management professor at the University of North Carolina's Kenan-Flagler School of

Business, surveyed 775 people. Men and women equally reported that they had been targets of what Ms. Pearson described as "rude, insensitive, discourteous behavior" at the office. The people they described as the instigators were, on average, about seven years older than their victims, mostly male, and usually higher up on the corporate totem pole.

In many cases nothing was intended, but it happened because people get into too much of a hurry. My friend and mentor Fred Smith says we need to remember that in most cases when people are rude and unkind to us, it doesn't mean they want to hurt us or that they're even angry with us. It does, in many cases, mean they're hurting. Quite often the other person is under a considerable amount of pressure and perceives his target as a threat to his own job security.

There's a good chance that part of the short-answer syndrome, or downright rudeness, is an indirect spin-off from road rage. Perhaps a traffic jam caused by a wreck or an unexpected rainfall or snow, or someone crawling along in the passing lane and stalling traffic behind them, got their dander up. Some workers arrive late and are under intense pressure to complete assignments. Consequently, they take a no-nonsense approach and have little empathy for others who are also tardy or behind in their responsibilities. This is especially true when management changes occur, a takeover threat looms ahead, downsizing happens, budget reductions are announced, etc.

The seriousness of this problem is pointed out in a *Dallas Morning News* article that stated that new research indicates that "rudeness, in addition to being a distracting irritant to the worker, can affect the company's bottom line by reducing productivity and leading to costly worker turnover." The article went on to say that "academics and industrial psychologists use a number of terms to describe the phenomenon: workplace incivility, counterproductive behavior, workplace aggression, personality conflict, workplace mistreatment, interpersonal deviance, bullying, mobbing. 'There are so many terms, I'm keeping a running list,' said social psychologist Loraleigh Keashly, an associate professor of urban and labor studies at Wayne State University in Detroit."

> *"Vulgar of manner, overfed, Overdressed and underbred; Heartless, Godless, hell's delight, Rude by day and lewd by night."*
> **—Byron Rufus Newton**

Another factor may be that our cultures are being blended more and more, and it's occasionally difficult to understand the speech of others. This slows the tempo, and in some cases when words are not understood, we have to ask the other person to repeat himself or herself several times, causing further irritation and sometimes anger.

So what's the solution? Basically, it's to "lighten up," to remember that the entire world is not revolving around what happens on your job today. A pleasant smile and a good attitude make a big difference. Research shows that if everybody read newspaper comic strips before they left home and listened to some recorded jokes, inspirational tapes, or soothing music as they drove, they'd arrive in a better frame of mind.

Additionally, as Mama Ziglar said, "Everybody can't be the smartest person in town, but all of us can be courteous and considerate of the other person." A little courtesy, mixed in with a pleasant smile and a cheerful attitude, will diffuse a lot of people with short fuses. Courtesy could help you avoid serious problems, secure your job, and bring a promotion as well.

Message!

Common courtesy benefits everyone and enriches our personal and professional lives. The Golden Rule—treat others like you want to be treated—is the best human relations rule known to man.

$---$ *32* $---$

WINNERS DON'T ALWAYS COME IN FIRST

Winners sometimes don't even come in second! I'm thinking of Dan Foresman, the outstanding PGA touring professional who, in the 1993 Master's Tournament, was within one stroke of the eventual winner, Bernhard Langer. They had seven holes

> *"Do not tell me how hard you work. Tell me how much you get done."*
> **—James J. Ling**

to play on the back nine, so it was still anybody's tournament. On the next hole Dan stepped up to the tee and proceeded to dump a ball into the water. Then he knocked a second ball into the water and ended up with a disastrous seven on a tough par three hole. The reality was that the tournament victory itself was out of his reach. But being the professional he is, Dan Foresman responded to the disaster and birdied two of the next three holes. He eventually ended up in a tie for fifth place.

I insist that Dan Foresman was a winner because instead of blowing up, and perhaps ending up in fiftieth place, he responded in a positive manner and played better the rest of the round. Later he said he learned a great deal about himself as a result of it and felt he was a better person and a better player.

I believe Dan Foresman probably learned his winning attitude when he was a child. I imagine his parents helped him know his worth by supporting him, encouraging him when he was frustrated, and by being honest about how well he was doing. There is nothing more cruel than telling a child he is gifted in something when he clearly is not. Two things happen in that case: Either the child is ridiculed, and consequently heartbroken, by other children when his lack of true talent is exposed, or the child grows up offering to share his talent (I'm specifically thinking of singing or playing an instrument), and everyone is horrified and embarrassed for the person when he performs but no one has the heart to tell him how bad he is. Gentle redirection of a child's interests can save the child's self-esteem and help him find something he can excel in.

There are those who scoff at the old saying that "it's not whether you win or lose, but how you play the game that counts." In my judgment, that's a true statement. Life is a big game made up of many smaller games, and how you play those little games does make a difference. To the participating athlete, the particular contest he's involved in is not necessarily a little game. But compared to all of life, he would have to put it in that category. But the way you play each part of your life is certainly a part of the whole.

"In my mind, talent plus knowledge, plus effort account for success."
—**Gertrude Samuels**

Even today I read in the newspaper that Andre Agassi defeated Pete Sampras in one of the grand-slam events in Australia. Everything indicates it was one of those classics, a five-set duel that showed both players at their very best. Agassi prevailed in this particular match, but there is no question in anyone's mind that not only could it have gone either way, but that each player was near the top of his game and gave it everything he had. To say that Sampras is the "loser" would simply do a great player with a big heart and a tremendous game an incredible disservice.

On the other hand, to deny the fact that Agassi—that day—was the winner of a historic match would deny him the reality of a hard-fought victory well earned. I have an idea that both men slept better and each feels good about himself because of the tremendous effort he expended and the fact that each was doing his best. Yes, in my book, that's what makes a winner. I believe that when we give it our best shot we emerge winners, regardless of the final score.

Message!

When you give anything your best effort,
you emerge a winner.

— 33 —

LOOKS CAN BE DECEIVING

One afternoon I was working in my office when the doorbell rang. Taffy, my little Welsh Corgi, answered, barking with his customary enthusiasm while rushing for the front door.

At first glance from the top of the stairway, I thought it was my granddaughter, the one I call "Keeper." When I

opened the door, there stood a tall, attractive young woman, blonde with a tinge of red in her hair.

With a great big smile and lots of enthusiasm, she told me that our next-door neighbor had suggested she come by. She indicated that she represented a charitable group and was working on winning a trip to London by selling magazines that would be sent to children's hospitals for the children to enjoy. She suggested that we "probably had more magazines than we had time to read anyhow."

I invited her to come in and explain the offer. Frankly, there were so many magazines, and I really don't know all of the magazines children enjoy reading, so I asked about whether the advice they contained would be of an ethical, moral, spiritual base. She assured me that the magazines had been carefully selected and were offered in groups that met my criteria.

I thought the price was a little high, but it was for a good cause, so I said OK. As she was finishing the paperwork, my wife returned. Fortunately, she is not as gullible as I am, and she started asking questions. The girl explained that she was so-and-so's daughter, who was a friend of ours, and added that the next-door neighbor had sent her over because she knew we loved children. After more questions, my wife said OK and wrote the check. Then her "women's intuition" kicked in. She was not comfortable with the transaction, so she called our next-door neighbor, who informed her that the young woman had said we sent her to see them. This was disturbing—to say the very least. My experience has been that those who lie to you about one thing will lie to you about other things.

I wish I could have talked with the girl again. I would have pointed out that she was on a slippery slope and that she would never enjoy any peace of mind or permanent success by deceiving, lying, misleading, and stealing from other people. I would have warned her that one con job leads to another and that the time she spent looking over her shoulder would keep her from establishing herself in a reputable organization or business. I would also have told her that her lifestyle would keep her from being attractive to the kind of man who would make a good mate to travel through life with.

> *"No one becomes depraved in a moment."*
> **—Decimus Junius Juvenal**

I don't know if my talk would have had any bearing on her conduct, but I really do wish I had had the opportunity to share those things with her.

Because we do have concern for other people, and especially those who are our neighbors, we called the neighborhood crime patrol and alerted them to the fact that our area had once again been targeted for a scam. My wife, being the action-oriented member of the family, took the receipt, called the magazine company, and reported the incident to them.

My message to you is this: Be careful. Just because a person looks good and sounds good is not necessarily proof that he or she is good. Evaluate the transaction by evaluating the person. To be candid, I'm glad my wife got home when she did. Otherwise, we would be out the dollars and the young lady would have gotten away with another fraudulent scheme. Too bad. With her personality and obvious intelligence, she could do well in life if she were on the right path. The path she's on will lead her nowhere, except into more trouble.

Message from Mama Ziglar!

"Tell the truth and tell it ever, costeth what it may, for he who hides the wrong he did, does the wrong thing still."

34

YOU CAN BE HAPPIER

Ask the average person what he or she would like to be, and many will say they just want to be happy—happy in their home, job, and life. To many people, happiness seems "the impossible dream," yet there are several things each of us can do to be more happy.

The first thing everyone can do to achieve happiness is to come to the realization that they have the sole responsibility for

> *"If happiness is activity in accordance with excellence, it is reasonable that it should be in accordance with the highest excellence."*
> **—Aristotle**

their happiness. The bride or groom who believes that it is his or her mate's responsibility to keep him or her happy is in for years of bitter disappointment. Self-centeredness is the by-product of years of living life as a single, so it is not uncommon for couples to enter marriage with this attitude: "I will ask not what I can do for my mate but only what my mate can do for me." Making your mate's happiness your highest priority—even though you are not responsible for it—will make both of you happier.

Dr. Michael Guillen points out, "Some of us are wired for singing the blues and others for singing in the rain." Several studies reveal that regardless of what your natural bent is, you can change from optimism to pessimism and vice versa. When you reach the age of accountability, you can choose to be optimistic or pessimistic unless there is a chemical imbalance—which you can choose to get treatment for. Feed your mind joyful songs, exciting information, and things that make you laugh or smile, and you have chosen to be optimistic and feel happier in the process. Dr. David Myers says that "happiness is chronic." Research shows that people who several years ago said they were "very unhappy" or "happy" tend to state much the same thing today, despite changing circumstances in their lives.

So what do we do to switch over to, as Dr. Guillen puts it, "the happiness thermostat"? He says, "Scientists suggest to start by exercising, getting plenty of sleep and smiling." He says these simple acts seem to trigger the release of powerful antidepressants like serotonin and dopamine. "It might make your brain begin to glow, and who knows, even make you feel like giggling." Dr. Guillen also points out that happiness has an effect on your body and that the latest studies show that if you're depressed you have a four times greater chance of having a heart attack.

Research shows that in happy people they find the "killer T-cells" in their immune system far more active than others, and that those T-cells are what fight disease. They also say that optimists seem to recover much faster from major surgery. In other words, happiness is good for your health. Optimistic people live longer. He also points out that happy people are ones who have goals and are working toward something, and that exercise is a mild anti-depressant.

There are other factors involved in all of this, but one thing that contributes to happiness is the fact that you are growing. You are learning things today that are important for your life tomorrow. Any feeling of accomplishment increases not only your happiness but also your confidence, which improves your performance, which makes you more successful in all areas of life—which makes you happier. Accept responsibility for your own happiness, make the commitment to take the necessary steps, and you can at least be happier—which is a big step toward being happy.

> *"I believe in one God and no more, and I hope for happiness beyond this life. I believe in the equality of man; and I believe that religious duties consist in doing justice, loving mercy, and endeavoring to make our fellow-creatures happy."*
> **—Thomas Paine**

Message!

Happy people feel that regardless of what happens today, tomorrow will be better.

---- *35* ----

LITTLE THINGS MATTER

"But if one should guide his life by true principles, man's greatest wealth is to live on a little with contented mind; for a little is never lacking."
—*Titus Lucretius Carus*

The history of our country involves every generation looking for the "pot of gold at the end of the rainbow." Many of them looked by digging in the hillsides and streams of America for gold.

In 1848 John Marshall was panning for gold in the streams of California. One bright, sunlit day while panning in Sutter's Creek, his eye caught a glitter—and the gold rush of 1849 was on. Many people came to California, discovered gold, and made their fortunes, while others struck it rich by providing mining equipment, food, shelter, clothing for the miners at exorbitant prices, so they found their gold in the pockets of those who had dug it up. The gold rush had a significant impact on the population of California and hastened the settling of our country.

In the late 1880s in an isolated, abandoned mine shaft about an hour's drive from where the gold had been discovered, the body of a derelict miner was found. It was John Marshall, the man who had discovered the gold but neglected to file his own claim. That's the story of life for many people.

Many of us know someone who neglected some little thing and ended up with the short end of the stick. Little things make a big difference in life. Sometimes a life is saved because the rescuer arrives in the nick of time. In a recent flash flood in California, two young men were pulled from a raging river by rescuers who, with the aid of a helicopter, lifted them out of the water. One of the rescuers said, "Had we been thirty seconds later, they would have lost their lives." In many instances had the police arrived at a scene two minutes later, rape and possibly murder would have occurred. In other cases we've seen where rescuers arrived a moment or two late and lives were lost.

However, the little things I'm talking about are not quite that traumatic, and yet in many ways have tremendous importance. The definition of *little* in my 1828 Noah Webster dictionary simply says that it is "small in size or extent, not great or large. Short in duration, as a little time, a little sleep. Slight; inconsiderable; not much." Now, tie the word *little* to *kindness,* and we see its significance. In Ephesians 4:32, we read, "Be kind to one another, tender-hearted, forgiving one another." *Kind* or *kindness* means "favorable; attractive; disposed to do good to others and to make them happy by granting their requests, supplying their wants, or assisting them in distress." Take the definition of *little* and apply the word *kind* or *kindness* to it, and we can see that a little kindness goes a long way toward encouraging people, building winning relationships, and giving them hope and inspiration in their daily lives.

> *"Beauty in things exists in the mind which contemplates them."*
> **—David Hume**

Yes, little things can make a huge difference. If you're only three minutes late for a flight, the three minutes is not much; but if the plane has left the ground it could have serious repercussions on your travel schedule.

Wilhelm Reiss, a German inventor, perfected a device for transmitting sound over wires. Had he moved two electrodes just one one-thousandth of an inch, they would have touched each other and he would have been the inventor of the telephone. That little bit of distance made all the difference!

Most of us need a little hope and encouragement every day. I believe a National Kindness Day, to encourage everyone to speak with kindness to those we meet, would help.

Doing that for just one day could jump-start us to make it a part of our lives, which could encourage others to do the same thing.

Message!

Stake your claim on what you want out of life. Get busy immediately doing the right thing in the right way in a series of ongoing "little" steps, and the day will come when what you "claimed" will be yours.

— 36 —

PUT IT BEHIND YOU

"Never look down to test the ground before taking your next step: only he who keeps his eye fixed on the far horizon will find his right road."

—Dag Hammarskjöld

All of us have "skeletons in our closets" and I'm convinced that none of us would want everything we've done exposed in the media. Fortunately, most people take steps to right wrongs and remove hidden skeletons in the closets of their past. Unfortunately, many times we neglect to forgive ourselves and recognize that the past is exactly that—the past. All of us have the opportunity to let our past either teach us or beat us. The choice is ours.

An anonymous writer put it this way: "There comes a time when we must clean out the closets of our lives so that we may have room for items that will enhance our lives. Let's search the closets of our lives and make a trip to the wastebasket. Throw away any hatred that may be lurking there, and be sure to toss out jealousy, bad attitudes, dishonesty, complaints, sin and hypocrisy. Before you finish, throw away that grudge you've been carrying against someone. Make room to add love, honesty, forgiveness and kindness, not to mention thankfulness for all of God's blessings. Go and make room for reverence and respect for God, from Whom all good comes. Stand back and look. Your life's closet is looking better, isn't it? Take a moment today to spring clean your heart. Ask God to come in and if He finds anything else that should not be there, to take it out so that you can live holy and right."

> *"Sometimes a noble failure serves the world as faithfully as a distinguished success."*
> **—Edward Dowden**

For many years I've made the observation that you've got to clean up your past so you can focus on the present. This will help guarantee a better and brighter future. Part of dealing with the past is the commitment to live with integrity today. This makes certain the closet does not accumulate more skeletons and create even more problems in the future. Living with integrity means that you do the right thing. By doing that you will eliminate any future guilt. When you remove both fear and guilt from your shoulders, your burden is lighter and you can make much better progress in your future.

Not only that, but the future could include moving up into leadership positions. Emerson said, "If you would lift me up, you must be on higher ground." My dictionary says that guilt is a debt contracted by an offense, a fine. The next part of the definition, however, actually gives encouragement: "To constitute guilt there must be a moral agent enjoying freedom of will and capable of distinguishing between right and wrong."

In short, when we recognize that we have done wrong and decide to make restitution, it's a sign that we have moral values, and that's important for our future. By cleaning up the guilt associated with the past, then and only then are we able to focus on the present. And what you do in the present will determine just how big and productive your future will be.

Carl Bard puts this all in perspective when he says, "Though no one can go back and make a brand new start, anyone can start from now and make a brand new ending." In many ways this is the major benefit of character, which is the foundation stone upon which all long-term positive relationships are built. Arthur Friedman says, "Men of genius are admired. Men of wealth are envied. Men of power are feared. But only men of character are trusted." It makes sense to deal with the past in order to enrich our lives and give us the freedom to be the best we can be.

Message!

_Guilt, anger, and fear are heavy burdens to carry. Doing the
right thing eliminates guilt. Acting with integrity eliminates the
fear of being "found out" because you have nothing to hide.
With the albatross of fear and guilt removed, you can travel
faster go farther and have more fun on the trip._

— *37* —

GOOD ADVICE

Dr. Tony Zeiss is president of Piedmont Community College in Charlotte, North Carolina, which serves seventy thousand students every year. His civic involvement, church commitments, family responsibilities, and corporate boards also keep him a very busy man.

His book *The Nine Essential Laws for Becoming Influential,* contains real gems of wisdom. With his permission I'm including some of those gems in hopes you will acquire your own copy of the book.

One of his important laws for becoming influential is the law of having a strong work ethic. He says you can verify the truth of this important law by answering the following questions:

"If I'm paying someone to paint my house, do I want the painter to do a quick job, a mediocre job, or a thoroughly professional job including cleanup?

"If I'm paying someone by the hour to repair my automobile, how often would I want him to take breaks or chat with coworkers?

"When I've employed someone to repair my plumbing, do I expect it to be halfway, mostly or totally fixed?"

He goes on to say that your answers are the same as everybody else's. We expect to get our money's worth from people we pay to render a service. After all, businesses are owned and operated by people just like the rest of us. American businessmen and businesswomen recognize that people make their businesses successful or unsuccessful, and that is why training and work ethic are so important to them.

Another of Dr. Zeiss's laws is the law of teamwork. He quotes an anonymous source that says, "If you don't believe in cooperation, just observe what happens to a wagon when one wheel comes off." Then, as always, he has some questions:

"Have I ever seen an effective organization that did not have a common purpose and good teamwork by its members?

"Is it possible for me to build a Delta II Rocket by myself?

"How many loners have I really enjoyed working around?"

Dr. Zeiss then shares an experience he had working with a brilliant man who could have accomplished almost anything as long as no one got in his way. People marveled at his passion for life and for his work. His peers appreciated his talent and admired his innovative ideas. His superiors (and Tony was one of them) loved his work as an individual, but they were constantly worried about who he would offend next. Unfortunately, this talented person could not work well with any ideas except his own. In consequence, he often felt it necessary to confront others about their "lousy ideas" and "stupid opinions." "Poor fellow," writes Dr. Zeiss, "the last I knew he was jumping from job to job and being completely misunderstood and unappreciated."

> *"Life is very short, and the quiet hours of it few, we ought to waste none of them in reading valueless books."*
> —**John Ruskin**

We once had a fellow working with us who, too, was "brilliant," could handle complex problems rapidly, and was generally right. But he managed to offend virtually every person he met. As a matter of fact, much like the old "Li'l Abner" comic strip, there was a cloud that hung over his head. Wherever he went, gloom and doom generally followed. He could do the work of three people. Unfortunately, he delayed the work of a dozen others. I have no idea where this person is now. But unless he developed a team spirit and started working on his relationship skills, he is still moving from one job to the next.

I encourage you to pick up a copy of this little book by Tony Zeiss, *The Nine Laws for Becoming Influential*

(Tulsa, OK: Triumphant Publishers International, 2000). It won't take long to read, and it's loaded with ideas and directions.

Message!

You must "get along" with others or "go along" a lonely road of frustration and disappointment, wondering why "they" can't see "it" your way.

THIS TIGER
REALLY ROARS

> *"Conduct is three-fourths of our life and its largest concern."*
> **—Matthew Arnold**

For several years America and the world have been enthralled by the golf exploits of Tiger Woods. His victories in the three majors stamped him with an unbeatable image. Indeed, that is the way it appeared when he won the U.S. Open by a record fifteen strokes.

Question: How did he do it, and what lessons can we learn from him, whether we play golf or not? Let's start at the beginning. Tiger was obviously born with a great athletic talent and parents who loved him, believed in him, and encouraged him. His father, Earl, was an excellent amateur golfer and taught his son to love the game. I've seen film clips of Tiger at age three, and even then what he could do with a golf club was astonishing. On his way to the pro ranks he broke virtually every record for young golfers, teenage golfers, and college golfers. He signed multimillion-dollar sponsoring contracts before he entered his first professional tournament. Not only was he blessed with great ability and great parents who guided him along the way, but Tiger Woods was also gifted with the desire to learn and a passion for the game.

Now let's pause and review. First, great inherent natural ability. Second, parents who also served as mentors. Third, a passion for golf. Fourth, a great work ethic. That approach gets you off to a good start whether you want to be a physician, salesperson, or government official.

Perhaps the most significant point to make is that after his overwhelming victory in his first Masters as a pro, which he won by twelve strokes—the biggest victory margin in Masters history—he proceeded to retool his swing. That's unheard of in the game of golf. An overwhelming victory and you retool your swing? But the experts were fairly unanimous in their agreement that on a wide-open course like the Masters, his bombs-away approach was fine; but on the tighter courses for the PGA Tournament, and certainly for the British and U.S. Opens, that approach wouldn't work. He engaged Butch Harmon, the man many considered the reigning king of teachers in the game of golf, to be his personal coach.

Whatever your field of endeavor, mentoring is an important part of what you do. If there has ever been a young man with the world at his feet, untold riches at his disposal, an opportunity to make a difference in the lives of many people and be a role model for all young people aspiring for greatness, it's Tiger Woods.

> *"It takes twenty years to build a reputation and five minutes to ruin it."*
> —*Warren Buffett*

Except for a fly in the ointment—language control—he's the consummate professional in his chosen field. Many people don't think it's important, but what comes out of your mouth reveals what's inside. On the eighteenth hole in the third round of the U.S. Open at Pebble Beach, Tiger hooked his drive, and the ball ended up on the beach. The language that followed would be an embarrassment to any person who values clean speech. I'm sad to say this is not the only instance where his use of "unfortunate" language has been recorded. Fortunately, he's young, and he does listen to his advisers. If he responds and makes the adjustment to control his language, he not only has an unlimited future for himself, but his influence will expand far beyond the world of golf.

Message!

You must learn to manage yourself in each area of your life in order to lead others and be all you are capable of being.

— 39 —

LITTLE EXTRAS MAKE A BIG DIFFERENCE

Art Linkletter is truly an icon in American history. He's over ninety years old and he's still radiant, swims twenty-six laps every day, eats sensibly, neither smokes nor drinks, and enjoys life as much as anyone I know. He goes to his office every day at ten o'clock and stays until three, contacting, managing, and working with the various

"This is the hardest of all: to close the open hand out of love, and keep modest as a giver."
—Friedrich Wilhelm Nietzsche

companies he has around the world. I don't believe the word *retirement* is in Art's vocabulary.

Art gives us this marvelous advice: "Do a little more than you are paid to, give a little more than you have to, try a little harder than you want to, aim a little higher than you think possible, and give a lot of thanks to God for health, family, and friends."

Let's take Art's marvelous observations and explore them a little deeper. "Do a little more than you're paid to" is good advice, regardless of how "menial" your job might be. Colin Powell, former chairman of the Joint Chiefs of Staff, got his first job mopping floors at a Pepsi-Cola plant. He resolved he was going to be better at it than anybody had ever been before. That became his trademark for all of his life. It's true that "when you do more than you're paid to do, the day will come when you'll be paid more for what you do."

"Give a little more than you have to." All of us have heard about "going the extra mile," but people seem to have lost sight of the energizing impact of giving to others. Giving more than you have to is always a friend-making, career-building, family-solidifying approach that psychologists say energizes you physiologically. I'm proud to point out that Americans are among the most charitable people in the world, giving freely of their time and money.

When Art says to "try a little harder than you want to," he's challenging you to be your best self. It's true that everyone has resources they have not tapped. All of us have heard about "the second wind," but psychologists have validated that we also have a third, fourth, and even fifth wind. I can tell you as a former jogger (I'm now a fast walker) that on many occasions I did not "feel like" I could go another fifty steps, much less another half mile. Much to my delight, many times when I added that other little bit I was reenergized and able to go twice as far as I thought I could.

"Aim a little higher than you think possible" is sound advice. Personal trainers will tell you that the problem most people have when they work out on weights by themselves is that they don't believe they can lift as much

> *"Our wishes lengthen as our sun declines."*
> —**Edward Young**

weight as they can, so they minimize and slow their progress. It is easier to achieve more when someone you respect is encouraging you, reassuring you, and cheering you on to a higher level of performance. You can teach yourself to be your own best cheerleader by always considering the possibility of aiming a little higher.

Finally, Art says, "Give a lot of thanks to God for health, family, and friends." We often take our health for granted until it is too late. Surely we should be grateful enough for our health to take Art's advice and eat sensibly, exercise regularly, and thank God for our good health. Many times we also take our family and friends for granted until something happens, either through death, divorce, a move, etc. Research indicates that the closer we get to our families, the more effective we will be in our careers. And the bottom line is, "The more you thank God for what you have, the more you will have to thank God for."

Message!

Do more, give more, try harder, aim higher, and give thanks.
The rewards will be yours.

40

THE DIVINE PIG

An article in *The Pittsburgh Post-Gazette* of October 15, 1998, by Michael A. Fuoco tells an amazing story in what is truly one of the most unusual incidents I've ever read about. In a condensed version, here's what happened:

> *"It is circumstance and proper timing that give an action its character and make it either good or bad."*
> —**Agesilaus**

Mrs. Joann Altsman did not have any idea when she agreed to take in a Vietnamese potbellied pig and keep her for a few days for her daughter that Lulu would be the instrument that would literally save her life. On August 4, Lulu did something that the fictional Lassie could never equal in all the years she appeared on television and the innumerable times she came to the rescue. I make this Lassie observation because even though Mrs. Altsman has an American Eskimo dog that barked at her after she collapsed and tried to summon help by breaking a bedroom window—

quite an amazing story on its own—Lulu the pig did much, much more.

Mrs. Altsman, who'd had a heart attack eighteen months earlier, started yelling for somebody to help her and call an ambulance. Lulu, seeing that she was crying, then started crying. According to Mrs. Altsman, Lulu shed big, fat tears. But then Lulu pulled herself together and headed outside through the doggy/piggy door and into the fenced yard. Please understand that Lulu had never left the confines of a yard, except for a leashed walk, but she knew that what had happened was something out of the ordinary. Somehow she opened the gate and walked into the road. According to witnesses, there Lulu gave new meaning to the phrase "hogging the road."

Later, Mrs. Altsman said that Lulu waited until a car approached and then walked into the road and lay down in front of it. Finally, a motorist stopped for the prone pig and got out. Lulu at that point knew just what she had to do. She led the driver to the house and the rescue. Mrs. Altsman said, "I heard a man yelling through the door, 'Lady, your pig's in distress!'" Then Mrs. Altsman replied, "No, I'm in distress! Please call an ambulance." And a few minutes later the ambulance appeared.

When they arrived the paramedics administered help immediately. When they loaded Mrs. Altsman into the ambulance, Lulu tried to join them, but the medics told her she had done enough for the day and she could now stay home. It wasn't until some time later that they realized Lulu had cut her stomach when she squeezed through the small doggie/piggie door.

This makes for quite an amazing story. But there is something I can't overlook and simply must add to this story. As a Christian, I believe the Bible is the inspired Word of God. In Psalm 139:16, we are told that our days are numbered even before we are born. It wasn't Mrs. Altsman's time to

> *"The most beautiful thing we can experience is the mysterious. It is the source of all true art and science."*
> —**Albert Einstein**

go. But God once again demonstrated his compassion, love, and resourcefulness when, of all things, he sent a Vietnamese potbellied pig to be the instrument for Mrs. Altsman's survival. The paramedics said had they been just fifteen minutes later she probably would have died.

I also believe God was involved simply because there are too many coincidences in this story. Mrs. Altsman was supposed to have kept Lulu five days. Then her daughter asked her to keep her another weekend, then another week, and then another, and yet another. The doggie/piggie door had already been enlarged a couple of times. Had it not been enlarged the last time, maybe Lulu could not have gotten through. Somebody once said that coincidence is God's way of staying anonymous. I'm sure Mrs. Altsman is glad that anonymous or not, he sent Lulu to the rescue.

Message!

The words "dumb animal" certainly don't apply here. In addition to Lulu's innate intelligence, she demonstrated compassion, empathy, persistence, creativity, selflessness, sympathy, determination—and best of all, love. Those are qualities which even people could use to the benefit of others.

—— *41* ——

THE ORPHAN WHO MADE GOOD WITH HAMBURGERS

Everyone reading this probably already knows that the late Dave Thomas was the founder of Wendy's Old Fashioned Hamburgers. His grandfatherly appearance on television helped make him extraordinarily effective at representing his own company. Chances are also great that you know he was an orphan and was adopted. But there is much more to the story than that.

It seems that from the time he was about eight years old Dave knew he wanted to be in the hamburger business.

> *"If a man has a talent and cannot use it, he has failed. If he has a talent and uses only half of it, he has partly failed. If he has a talent and learns somehow to use the whole of it, he has gloriously succeeded, and won a satisfaction and a triumph few men ever know."*
>
> **—William Lindsay White**

But before he got there, he cooked just about everything but hamburgers, including chicken and fish and chips. Born on July 2, 1932, in Atlantic City, New Jersey, Dave never knew his parents. He was adopted by a couple from Kalamazoo, Michigan, when he was six weeks old. Unfortunately, his adoptive mother died when he was just five years old. From that point on he moved from state to state as his adoptive father sought work.

When he was fifteen, his family moved to Fort Wayne, Indiana, and Dave got a job as a bus boy at the Hobby House Restaurant. Later, when his family moved again, Thomas made a life-impacting decision. He decided to stay where he was, took a room at the YMCA, and continued to work long, hard hours at the restaurant. As a result, he dropped out of school after completing only the tenth grade. When he was eighteen he decided to join the Army and attended the Army's cook and baker school before he served a tour of duty in Frankfurt, Germany. Here he became one of the youngest soldiers ever to manage an enlisted men's club.

Upon his discharge he returned to the Hobby House as a short-order cook. Here he met his future wife, Lorraine, a waitress. They were married in 1954. In 1962 he joined Kentucky Fried Chicken and moved four bankrupt take-out stores in Columbus, Ohio, into a $1.5 million personal profit. He was a millionaire at age thirty-five. After he left Kentucky Fried Chicken, he helped found Arthur Treacher's Fish & Chips. But Dave was hooked on the idea that the hamburger business was where he wanted to be. He opened his first Wendy's on November 15, 1969, in downtown Columbus. He named his restaurant after his eight-year-old daughter, Melinda Lou, who was called Wendy by her brother and sisters.

> _"The great secret of success in life is for a man to be ready when his opportunity comes."_
> **—Benjamin Disraeli**

Initially his ambition was modest. He did hope some day to have several restaurants around Columbus that would provide a place for his children to work in the summer. But his dreams expanded as his restaurants caught on, not only in Columbus but in other areas of the country. Today there are several thousand franchises, and Wendy's seems to have a limitless future for expansion.

But the thing that set Dave Thomas apart was his consistency. He believed that hard work, patience, and honesty are the bedrock for permanent success in the business world as well as home and personal life. He also knew that commitment makes the difference in success or failure for countless people.

If you've not made a commitment—whether it's in your marriage, your business, or even the pursuit of worthwhile civic goals—when you hit the roadblocks your first inclination is to look for ways to get out of the deal instead of ways to save it. We do find what we're looking for. The foundation stones of commitment and persistence upon which Dave Thomas built his empire will serve the rest of us well.

Message!

Dave Thomas had a dream, and the dream had him. His climb to the top involved many peaks and valleys, but his dream enabled him to scale the heights and leave a legacy.

--- *42* ---

OUR EDUCATIONAL
CHOICES

The June 2, 2000, issue of *USA Today* identified seventh-grader George Abraham Thampy as the best speller in the country. He won the $10,000 first-place prize, received a set of encyclopedias and a thousand-dollar savings bond. George correctly spelled "demarche" (a step or maneuver) to win the 2000 Scripps Howard National Spelling Bee in Washington, D.C. He tied for fourth place

> *"Those who seek education in the paths of duty are always deceived by the illusion that power in the hands of friends is an advantage to them."*
>
> **—Henry Brooks Adams**

in 1998 and finished in a third-place tie in 1999. But spelling is not George's only talent. A week earlier he placed second at the National Geography Bee, also in Washington, where he won $15,000. "It's not really the cash prizes and the trophies. It was really the words,"

George explained about why he returned to the spelling bee for the third time.

Both the runner-up, Sean Conley of Newark, California, and the third-place finisher, fourteen-year-old Alison Miller of Niskayuna, New York, are educated in the home, as is George. He says what makes homeschooling interesting to him is that his parents allow him to be flexible and give him the chance to study something else—like Latin.

Being given a choice about curriculum seems to work quite well for these kids. And when parents are qualified to teach, results nationwide validate that homeschooling works. This brings us to the next issue, giving parents vouchers so they can choose where they educate their children.

One of the reasons public schools are not doing as well as they otherwise could is because we have tied the hands of public school teachers and principals, many of whom are, under the circumstances, doing a marvelous job. Teachers are often required not to teach moral absolutes but rather to give children the choice about what is right for them. But most children develop educationally before they do emotionally. As a result, while kids might have the intelligence and knowledge to do well scholastically, they do not have the emotional maturity to make good choices.

I believe there is a reason why virtually every nation in the world sends sons and daughters to American colleges and universities to earn their sheepskins and frequently their master's degrees and Ph.D.s. However, very few of them send their children to our public schools to get their basic education. Reason: Monopolies seldom offer the most effective way to maximize results. Our public schools often have only token competition, although private and religious schools are growing by leaps and bounds.

> *"Public opinion's always in advance of the law."*
> —*John Galsworthy*

Academically speaking, colleges and universities say that their best students are those schooled at home, the second best are those who attended private schools, and the remainder hail from public schools. That's one of the reasons politicians, particularly those who live in the Washington, D.C., area, send their children to private schools. Yet some of them would deny the working parents in America the same privilege.

Study after study reveals that the majority of parents believe that given the opportunity they will make a responsible choice for their children. But the bureaucrats think the government is better qualified to make those decisions. The records indicate this is not true. Our schools simply are not turning out enough qualified candidates to fill the high-tech jobs that are available. Research by Central Piedmont Community College in Charlotte, North Carolina, validates that an estimated 340,000 unfilled positions for highly skilled workers go begging simply because not enough skilled workers are being produced through our schools and universities.

The good news is that the demand for vouchers is growing daily. Certainly parents in any state and city deserve the opportunity to see which is best, at least on a trial basis. The statistics will speak for themselves. Freedom of choice in education is certainly one of the primary issues in our society today. I hope you will let your elected representatives know where you stand on this issue.

Message!

Give choice a chance. Odds are long that competition would make public and private schools better. There's a reason a higher percentage of public school teachers send their children to private schools than does the general public.

--- *43* ---

THREE UNRELATED GEMS OF PERSEVERANCE

His name was Hal Wright, and he was the longtime publisher of a north Sierra newspaper. He gained fame by delivering papers to remote subscribers by tossing them out of his airplane. He died at age ninety-six after a short illness.

> *"Tis known by the name of perseverance in a good cause— and of obstinacy in a bad one."*
> **—Laurence Sterne**

In the midst of his fifty-year run as publisher and delivery service, he became a local and even a national celebrity, featured in the *London Daily Mail,* on CBS and *The Today Show,* as well as in *Ripley's Believe It or Not.* Both houses of the state legislature awarded him proclamations. Along the way Uncle Sam intervened, and Wright had to hire an attorney to force the

Federal Aviation Administration to renew his pilot's license. His newspaper, which was a major source of information to his subscribers, featured his own aerial photographs and tidbits of news from around Sierra County, which has a population of three thousand. He and his wife worked as a team. She was nicknamed "Sweetie Pie," and together they worked to publish the biweekly. They both qualify as gems.

The second gem is about a devoted mother and a way-too-small football player. This mother of several children was committed to keeping her family together when her husband died. She worked at several jobs doing menial tasks, everything from cleaning offices to delivering coal. Eventually she took the civil service exam and became the chief bookkeeper for the city treasurer. She used her strength and love to hold her family together and to raise her children.

One of the kids, though small, wanted to play football, but no college of any size offered him a scholarship. He played for a small college and excelled. Then his dream was to play in the NFL. He tried out for the Pittsburgh Steelers, which was his home team, but he was cut from the team in short order. Next he found a job in construction and helped build some of the skyscrapers seen today in Pittsburgh, but he held on to his dream. He did not see himself as a victim of circumstances but as a person who would succeed despite his size.

What he did was look at his options and decide he would start anywhere. He played in a little league that paid him six dollars a game and was able to improve his already considerable skills. He continued to stay in contact with NFL teams in hopes that he would be noticed. After seven months of trying, he received an invitation to try out for the Baltimore Colts . . . and I suppose that all of you football fans know the rest of that story. Johnny Unitas was one of the true greats and has been inducted into the NFL Hall of Fame. He was a real gem.

> *"Give us grace and strength to forbear and to persevere. Give us courage and gaiety and the quiet mind, spare to us our friends, soften to us our enemies."*
> —**Robert Louis Stevenson**

The third gem was a Texan who coined the phrase "Remember the Alamo!" Fortunately, he did a great deal more than that. Once on board a ship home from England, Gail Borden saw children die as a result of drinking contaminated milk. The experience impacted his mind forever. As a matter of fact, he dedicated the remainder of his life to finding a way for humans to drink milk safely. His experiments with condensed milk failed, but then one day he saw how the Shakers in New York condensed their maple sugar in a vacuum-sealed pan. His success led to the safety of milk in a non-refrigerated world, began the modern dairy industry, and launched a multibillion-dollar company. Yes, Gail

Borden was a true gem. On his tombstone are encouraging words of perseverance: "I tried and failed. I tried again and succeeded."

These three gems, each in its own way, teach some of life's greatest lessons.

Message!

Combine commitment, determination, perseverance, and a firm belief that you can beat the odds—and reach the impossible dream.

---— 44 ——

WELL-MEANING ADVICE

Recently a newspaper columnist was pre-sented with a problem. A young woman who was of good moral character, an excellent student, a respectful daughter, and an apparently all-around good person wrote seeking advice about her dilemma: Her father was never pleased with any-thing she did. He was always criticizing,

> "The advantage of doing one's praising for oneself is that one can lay it on so thick and exactly in the right places."
> —Samuel Butler

finding fault as if there were a reward for it, and, in general, repeatedly putting her down.

The columnist gave her this advice: Just ignore him and get on with your life. I believe that was poor advice. To advise someone to ignore a consistently faultfinding father is like advising someone to ignore a broken arm. There is a better way.

Eleanor Roosevelt said, "No one on earth can make you feel inferior without your permission. Just don't give it to them." Remember that you are somebody very special to God. This young woman undoubtedly means a great deal to her mother, and odds are good that she means much to her father, who is woefully short on human relationships skills.

This young woman surely knows her father has some good qualities or her mother would never have married him. Perhaps he's a good, steady provider, an honest and faithful husband. Maybe he loves his neighbor but doesn't know how to express his love for his daughter and encourage her positive qualities. I advise this young woman the next time her father criticizes her to smile and say, "You know, Dad, I never realized that I was not doing this better than I am. Thank you for telling me something for my own good. That's just one of the reasons I love you, Dad." Will this be easy? No, but keep reading.

Next, when she sees her father doing something like helping her mother with a household chore, coming home in time for dinner, or anything that shows he cares about his family, she should say to him, "Dad, that was really nice of you. I'll bet many families would appreciate a husband and father as thoughtful as you. That makes me proud to be your daughter."

When her dad walks in from work, she needs to welcome him home and say, "Dad, I'm glad you're home! Gimme a big ol' hug!" If her dad is not a hugger, that approach will soon make him one. Frankly, there are very few fathers who would not respond to warm, genuine hugs from their daughters.

Another step is a secondhand compliment. Example (make certain this is true!): She can say, "You know, Dad, I was telling one of my (coworkers/friends) today how attentive you are to the needs of our family, and how much we respect and appreciate you for that. Her comment was, 'He sounds like a really neat guy!'" or some-

"There is a moment of difficulty and danger at which flattery and falsehood can no longer deceive, and simplicity itself can no longer be misled."
—Junius

thing along those lines. By now his heart will be softening. Then she can spend a couple of bucks on a neat card (don't wait for Father's Day to do this!) and tell her dad, "I couldn't wait until Father's Day to give it to you. I wanted to see the smile on your face today."

My friend and mentor Fred Smith taught me long ago that most people who are mean, nasty, and ornery to you (as this young woman's father apparently was) do not do it because they want to hurt you—they do it because they are hurting. This approach will remove some of that hurt. The young woman has nothing to lose and a great deal to gain by trying it. I hope she sees what I've written and gives it a try because I'm convinced it will make a difference. I'm also convinced there are any number of readers who have the same basic situation, so this approach was also written for you.

Message!

Genuine love and respect manifested in sincere compliments and affection will, over a period of time, penetrate and melt the hardest heart.

45

POSITIONING IS IMPORTANT

Recently my wife and I enjoyed a meal at Chuck's, one of our special places to eat. Good food, great service, reasonable prices, and a fun atmosphere. As we were eating our lunch, my wife was distracted by some conversations going on around her, and I became intrigued with a game of pool on TV. Two female professionals were playing at it big time, and they were good—really good!

> *"Heaven gives its glimpses only to those Not in position to look too close."*
> **—Robert Frost**

As nearly as I could tell they were playing "rotation"—meaning they had to sink the balls in the order of their numbers. In this game, when you sink one shot in one of the pockets, you need to be in position to hit the next one. It requires considerable skill and concentration to hit the ball into a pocket and have the "cue" ball back up, roll forward, or bounce off the cushion—and it was a beautiful sight to see! In pool, positioning is everything. It doesn't take much skill to sink one shot if it's a straightaway. But hitting that shot in the pocket, then getting in position to hit the next one, is the key to winning.

As I watched, it occurred to me this is true of life. John Wooden, arguably the greatest basketball coach in history, taught his players that if a fellow player passed off the ball to you because you were in the best position to score, the one who did the scoring should always nod to the one who had passed him the ball. One day a player said to Wooden, "Suppose he's not looking?" Coach Wooden simply said, "He'll be looking."

That is life. First, we need to get into position. Second, when someone puts us in position to score, we need to acknowledge the favor because that puts us in position with our other teammates to receive more favors. That's not why you do it, but that's the way life works.

The things you say to one person today will either put you in position to be friends with that person or lose him or her as a friend, depending on your tone of voice and what you say. The attitude you bring to your job today will either put you in position to climb the ladder, or it will put you in position to be heading for the door. The foundation a youngster builds in his educational drive in those early years

After the orders were taken, the group was visiting and having a wonderful time swapping stories when one of the gentlemen, Peter Tricklebank from Australia, suggested they write an "I like . . . because" for Wendy. Since they had none of the forms with them, they improvised by using a napkin. Peter wrote his name and next to it wrote what he liked about Wendy. Then he passed it on to the others and one by one each participant wrote specific, observable behavior he or she liked about Wendy. The napkin was completely covered, front and back, and in addition each person attached his or her business card.

At the end of the meal the group asked Wendy to come back to the table. When she did, according to Gina, they presented her with the napkin and, to quote Gina, "The biggest smile I have ever seen spread across her face. She simply glowed." At that point, Gina said, they applauded Wendy for a good three minutes. All she could do was smile and laugh with sheer delight. On the way out, several people hugged her and thanked her for her outstanding service. "She was in tears as we were walking out the door. Once we were outside," according to Gina, "we were all incredibly pumped and full of excitement, talking about how incredible it felt and how powerful words are."

Gina said she assured everyone that Wendy would not remember the night before or the night after, but she

positions him or her for higher education and a successful career in business. When you learn how to do your own job properly, that puts you in position to teach someone else how to do the same job. And the way you move up the ladder, in most cases, is to be replacing yourself constantly—teaching, training, and inspiring others.

> *"To be loved, be lovable."*
> —**Ovid**

It works in your personal life, as well. The relationships you have with your family will put you in a position to have either a great attitude when you leave the house and prepare you for effectiveness on the job, or it could give you a lousy attitude and you might arrive in a bad mood. That takes you out of position to do your best work that day.

Everything builds on everything else. The words you say, the actions you take, the attitudes you develop, your friendliness, your spirit of cooperation and team play—all add up to putting you in a great position to continue to make progress in all areas of your life, or could take you out of the game. The thought should be, *What effect will this have on others?* When you think about it just for a moment, you can get in the habit of being the right kind of person—which puts you in position to do the right thing, which enables you to get more of the things life has to offer.

Message!

Every step or move you make has an impact on your future.
That's why you should weigh each step like the chess masters
do—by carefully considering what will happen down the road
as a result of your next move.

—— *46* ——

ENCOURAGING OTHERS HELPS YOU

I want to tell you about something that happened immediately thereafter as a direct result of what the participants learned in one of our special two-day "Born to Win" seminars.

When someone makes a contribution at "Born to Win," we encourage the others to write him or her a little note of encouragement on our "I like . . . because" pads. After this seminar was over, a group of eleven participants, including Gina Womack, who at that time was our associate support manager, went to the Trail Dust Steakhouse for dinner. reported that they had a really neat waitress named W who provided them with excellent service.

"I think no innocent species of wit or pleasantry should be suppressed; and that a good pun may be admitted among the smaller excellencies of lively conversation.
—James Bosw

guaranteed the others that in ten years she would remember that night. "One thing I know to be true is that I will remember that night as well," Gina concluded.

One of the things all people need virtually every day of their lives is a word of encouragement from somebody who says, "Well done." Wives need it from husbands, and husbands need it from wives. Children need it from parents—and yes, kids—parents need it from children. In our places of employment, "Good job," "Well done," "Thank you for being so effective," "I appreciate your promptness," or any word of encouragement that notes a specific, observable behavior can make an enormous difference in someone's life. Don't wait for Christmas, Thanksgiving, New Year's, birthdays, or anniversaries to do it because it's the right thing to do. You will feel good, the other person will feel good, and I suspect in many cases those "I like . . . becauses" will come at an important time in that person's life.

> *"We cannot tell the precise moment when friendship is formed. As in filling a vessel drop by drop, there is at last a drop which makes it run over; so in a series of kindnesses there is at last one which makes the heart run over."*
> —**James Boswell**

A lot of hurting is going on in our world, and we never know when a word of encouragement will brighten a person's day. I suspect Wendy will have a lot of days when she'll feel better because of that one night. I also believe she will show that napkin to friends, relatives, and perhaps even complete strangers! Put it in writing, and you'll be amazed at how impactful it can be. Commit to encouraging others, and I promise that you, too, will be encouraged.

Message!

Some people believe that compliments are just so much air. But when we remember that the tires on which we ride are filled with air and we consider how much smoother that makes our ride, we should start handing out more compliments.

—— 47 ——

A SLOW START IS NOT AN INDICTMENT

All of us are not born with equal opportunities. But over a period of time, regardless of our parentage, place of birth, prospects in our communities, or education, the day comes when we have to make the choice to let our past teach us—or beat us.

"Most barriers to your success are man-made. And most often, you're the man who made them."
—Frank Tyger

Some of us arrive in this world with physical handicaps, others with emotional handicaps, and still others without the benefit of an intact family. All of these are critical to an individual's success. Even with all of those things going against us, we still have the ultimate responsibility for taking control and doing something with our lives.

Winston Churchill, who was sixty years old before he gained respect and recognition, started life with a speech difficulty (he had a bad lisp and stuttered). He was a poor student, failing at least one grade, and once was the worst student in his class. This despite the fact that his father was an eloquent speaker and head of the House of Commons. Many thought Winston had not inherited a great deal from his father, and yet he will go down as one of the great speakers in history, not for his eloquence but for the content, sincerity, and conviction in what he said. He is often credited with saving the free world with his radio addresses to the British when the Nazis had overrun most of Europe and were poised to invade England.

Many of Thomas Edison's teachers thought he had a serious problem. He daydreamed in school and asked questions that appeared to have no significance. His mother took him out of school and educated him at home. He is recognized as the inventor who had the most impact on nineteenth-century America.

Clint Lewis from Magna, Utah, was born with poor eyesight, and after a few years he lost it completely. Today Clint Lewis is the wrestling coach at Brockbank Junior High School. In 2000, his team was undefeated and headed to the state championship matches. The exciting thing is that his wrestlers are seventh- and eighth-graders, and he has no students from the ninth grade. He is optimistic that the future will be even better for his teams.

When Clint was being considered for the wrestling coach's job, there was a lot of flak. The administration could not imagine, as Clint put it, "a blind guy teaching kids how to wrestle." But Clint is optimistic, upbeat, and very enthusiastic. He was a former state champion wrestler himself, even though he was blind, so his knowledge is considerable, and his optimism and positive thinking are even greater. And he loves to coach his kids.

"Success is the reward for accomplishment."
—**Harry F. Banks**

That's a winning combination in any language. Clint didn't get a good start, but it looks as if he's headed for a good ending.

There is a message in all of this, and it's primarily aimed at parents and teachers. The difficult student, or the child who does not respond early on, might be a shining star in later years. That's one of the reasons my mother never gave up on any of her children. Neither did she give up on any of her grandchildren. Her faith, belief, and encouragement had a huge impact on our lives.

The record books are filled with people who had reason to quit early on, but they received a word of encouragement, became persistent, and worked hard. They developed the characteristics of honesty, integrity, faith, love, loyalty, enthusiasm, commitment, and responsibility. They even learned to love and respect others, becoming difference-makers in the lives of many. So hang in there, parents and teachers. Encourage the young early in their lives. After all, it's not where you start—it's where you go that makes the difference. And perhaps most important of all, it's not what you get by succeeding in life—it's what you become by succeeding.

Message!

Hope is the foundational quality of all change, and encouragement is the fuel on which hope runs. Consistent words of encouragement will have a positive impact on the recipient.

48

THIS IS LOVE?

Over the past few years a common practice labels a child born out of wedlock as a "love child." What about children born *in* wedlock? Should these children feel that they are not "love children"?

To help clarify this, let's look at the definition of *love*. The dictionary identifies *love* as "an affection of the mind, excited by beauty and worth of any kind, or by the qualities of the object which communicates pleasure, sensual or intellectual. A strong affection for or attachment to another person based on regard or shared experiences or interests."

Dr. Joyce Brothers says that love is something we all yearn for and that to love and be loved is the most blissful state

"It is sometimes frightening to observe the success which comes even to the outlaw with a polished technique. . . . But I believe we must reckon with character in the end, for it is as potent a force in the world of conflict as it is in our own domestic affairs. It strikes the last blow in any battle."

—Philip D. Reed

imaginable. She says love is "caring as much for the aims and welfare of another person as you do about your own aims and well-being."

Dr. J. Allan Petersen lists four words describing love.

First is *stergo,* which he describes as the love parents have for their own children. This is the kind of love a parent has for offspring. It can be, and often is, sacrificial.

The second kind of love is *eros.* Although *eros* usually carries a negative connotation, it can be either good or bad. Its basis is primarily in the physical, triggered by emotion. *Eros* is the heart of sexual desire and romantic feelings.

Third is *phileo.* This kind of love is "a fondness or a liking based on similarity of outlook in life."

The fourth, and easily the most beautiful kind of love, is *agape.* Peterson saw this love culled out of one's heart by an awakened sense of value in the object loved that causes one to prize it. This love does not seek anything in return, not even acceptance of itself, but is first concerned for the other. It is the ultimate love, and it brings out the best in all of us.

Nearly two thousand years ago a Jewish scholar wrote his friends in Corinth and described real love. He said, "Love is patient, love is kind. It does not envy, it does not boast, it is not proud. It is not rude, it is not self-seeking, it is not easily angered, it keeps no record of wrongs. Love does not delight in evil but rejoices with the truth. It always protects, always trusts, always hopes, always perseveres. Love never fails" (1 Cor. 13:4–8 NIV). These definitions make it clear that the offspring of an adulterous relationship is not a "love child."

Will a child who is the result of this illicit relationship enjoy all the benefits which the children of real love share? Evidence is clear that this child will not have the benefits that other children have and enjoy. God will love her as much as he loves all the others, but this child will be burdened with a stigma through no fault of her own. How terribly sad.

Message!

Though "love child," a term which I believe was created out of "political correctness," is less harsh than the prior label given to children born out of wedlock, it is a label that romanticizes a very hurtful and harmful situation for a child. The real love children are those born to a husband and wife who raise them together, give them their name, and the best possible start for success in this life.

49

YOU ARE THE THIRD PERSON

"You, yourself, have got to see that there is no just interpretation of life except in terms of life's best things. No pleasure philosophy, no sensuality, no place nor power, no material success can for a moment give such inner satisfaction as the sense of living for good purposes, for maintenance of integrity, for the preservation of self-approval."

—Minot Simons

Several years ago I heard the statement that "every third person is either remarkably handsome and unusually bright, or amazingly beautiful and absolutely brilliant." I encourage you to make a mental note of this. The next two people you see, look them over real good. When you do, chances are excellent that you will come to the conclusion that it is neither one of them! That means it has to be you, if the formula is to hold true. When you think about it in these terms, I believe you will come to the conclusion that it does have to be you.

From this moment on I encourage you to think of yourself as that "third person."

As that third person, I want to share with you some important considerations about yourself. Several billion people have walked this earth, but there has never been, nor will there ever be, a person exactly like you. Your uniqueness gives you real value. Think about it like this: If man can take moldy bread and make penicillin out of it, think what an awesome God can make out of you. Listen to what St. Augustine said in A.D. 399 (and I paraphrase): Man travels hundreds of miles to gaze at the broad expanse of the ocean. He looks in awe at the heavens above. He stares in wonderment at the fields, the mountains, the rivers and the streams. And then he passes himself by without a thought—God's most amazing creation.

It is important that you think well, not egotistically, about yourself because the way you see yourself has a direct bearing on how you see and treat others. If you see yourself as happy, secure, self-sufficient, and as a good friend, you'll attract happy, secure, self-sufficient, good friends.

To get along well with people requires an elimination of prejudice, which, in virtually every case, is circumstantial, based either on ignorance or never having had any real relationship with those of a different race or culture. This does not mean that I'm suggesting or even mildly hinting that you have to agree with everybody on everything. To do so would be to invite disaster into your life. But it does mean that you can disagree without being disagreeable. You can disagree and yet respect the other person's right to believe as he or she believes. You can have a different opinion without denying the other person the right to have the opinion he or she has.

"Men who have attained things worth having in this world have worked while others idled, have persevered when others gave up in despair, have practiced early in life the valuable habits of self-denial, industry, and singleness of purpose. As a result, they enjoy in later life the success so often erroneously attributed to good luck."

—Grenville Kleiser

When you adopt that attitude and take that approach, you will probably be amazed to discover on occasion that your friend's point of view was right and yours was wrong. That's a sobering thought.

When you take the right attitude toward another person, you not only avoid building a wall between the two of you, but you also establish common ground and lay a solid foundation on which to build a relationship. It certainly is something to think about and something I have found to be very enlightening and beneficial. I encourage you to replay the tapes of your life and explore the number of times people who were "different" from you turned out to be really great people and had opinions with which you disagreed but that turned out to be correct. Take the approach I'm

Message!

When you change your "got to" to a "get to," you've moved up a step and are expressing gratitude. This is the healthiest of all human emotions.

51

INVESTING YOUR TIME

Most of us, with pen and paper, could figure out that there are 168 hours in a week. The way we invest those hours determines how happy, healthy, prosperous, and secure we are, how many friends and good family relationships we have, and how much peace of mind and hope are ours.

Health authorities tell us that we should get at least eight hours of sleep every night to maintain optimum health. Add to that eight hours of sleep a minimum of one hour a day preparing for bed and/or getting out of bed, showering, shaving, making up, dressing, etc. There goes nine hours each day, seven days a week, for a total of sixty-three hours! Most of us work eight hours a day and some many more than that, but for the person on an eight-hour day, getting to work, coming home from work, and winding down requires an additional hour, morning, and evening. So there goes ten hours a day, five days a week for a total of fifty hours. Already, 113 of our 168 hours are committed.

If we're honest we'll acknowledge that an hour is invested in each meal, not in the eating only but also in waiting to be seated, ordering, then waiting for the check or driving to and from the grocery store, shopping, preparing the food—there goes another 21 hours. Now we have used 134 hours, leaving us 34 of the 168 hours to spend with our families, exercise, socialize, devote to personal growth, relaxation, church, reading, doctor/dentist appointments, etc.

It makes sense for us to plan those hours or we will have no time for ourselves. We spend a great deal of time in pursuit of income to provide for our families. I frequently remind people that money is not the most important thing in life, but it is reasonably close to oxygen. It is needed to function in life. But how much do we need, and how many hours do we invest in pursuing those dollars?

Consider this: If all the gold in the world were melted down into a solid cube, it would be about the size of an eight-room house. But all that gold—billions of dollars' worth—could not buy a friend, character, peace of mind, a clear conscience, or a sense of eternity. All of this is to suggest that we should look carefully at where we are investing our time to see if we are going to end up at the end of life's road, look into the end zone, and be able to see many of the things money will buy and all of the things money won't buy. I believe if we will give this careful thought, we will replan, reevaluate, and perhaps change some of our priorities.

"Where ambition ends, happiness begins."
—Hungarian Proverb

Sheila Murray Bethel, a friend and fellow speaker, observed that she had never met a retired person or senior citizen who stated that if they had it to do over they would go to the office earlier, stay later, work harder, or do anything they could to climb higher and faster on the ladder of success. But she said she has met numerous people who said that if they had it to do over they would spend more time acquiring the things money won't buy and a little less time looking for the things that money will buy. In short, they were saying, "I'd spend more time with my family, take better care of my health, get involved in civic and community activities, make contributions to mankind in general."

That's a good game plan for life. A study reported in *Psychology Today* confirmed that those people who are active in the community doing good for others are so energized by it that they are more effective in their careers and, consequently, move even higher up the ladder.

Message!

When standard of living is your number one priority, your quality of life almost never goes up. If quality of life is your number one priority, your standard of living almost always goes up.

52

FROM PRISON TO NOBEL NOMINATION

"The world is given as the prize for the men in earnest."
—*Frederick W. Robertson*

Stanley Williams is the cofounder of the South Central Los Angeles Crips gang and was convicted of killing four people in 1981. Incredibly, Williams was nominated for a 2001 Nobel Peace Prize. It goes without saying that anyone who knew the Stanley Williams of "Crips" fame was stunned. So the question arises, especially since he is on death row, what has happened to move him from convicted murderer to Nobel Peace Prize nominee?

The amazing turnabout came through Barbara Becnel, executive director of Neighborhood House, a nonprofit community organization that runs a drug rehabilitation center, distributes free food, and offers other humanitarian services to its poor community. She met Williams in 1993 while researching an article on black youth gangs for *Essence* magazine. Her research led her to begin writing a book on the history of the Crips and their archrivals, the Bloods. She said that everywhere she went she was told she had to talk to "Big Took." Later she was to write that Stanley Williams was quite remorseful of his Crip legacy. She said he wanted to reverse his legacy. He told her he wanted to write children's books that preached an anti-gang message. They first worked together on a five-and one-half minute video message that was played at a summit between the Crips and the Bloods.

When it was all over, she said, "All four hundred people in the audience were at the edge of their seats. There was total silence. When the screen went dark, four hundred people leaped out of their chairs and started clapping. I thought if he could command that level of attention, maybe we were on to something."

Since then, many things have happened. Williams has written several books, most of which are subtitled, "Tookie Speaks Out Against Gang Violence." He has a brainchild, the Internet Project for Street Peace, which allows kids at North Richmond's Neighborhood House to talk to Somali immigrant children in Switzerland through E-mail and chat rooms, telling them how to avoid gangs and trouble.

Evelyn Nieves, writing for the New York Times News Service, tells of the old, dingy house that serves as an after-school center for the impoverished East Bay town of North Richmond, California, being alive with happy noise. She wrote, "Children crammed both floors, their presence masking the shabbiness. They pecked away on computer keyboards, sat at school desks finishing compositions and stuffed themselves into a corner room to hear Martika Pittman, 10, read from a book by an ex-gang leader now on death row: 'Many gang members think they respect themselves,' Martika read. 'They think they have good self-esteem because they feel good about themselves. But they are wrong. So were we.'"

> *"Genius is initiative on fire."*
> **—Holbrook Jackson**

Stanley "Tookie" Williams truly is an attention-grabber. He has aroused excitement among the kids who read and hear what he has to say. As word spread through the after-school center, the sixty children "came running from every which room to see if they, too, might talk to Tookie. 'Tookie! Tookie!' they shrieked, the way other children might react to Michael Jordan. 'Let me say hi!' 'No, let me!'"

He certainly is a big hit with the kids, and the fact that he was nominated for the Nobel Peace Prize screams that here is a man, despite all of his background, difficulties, problems, and violent crimes, who has decided to make a contribution to society. Only God knows what will happen, about whether or not his death sentence (he claims to be innocent) might be overturned. Regardless, he is going full speed ahead, doing what he can to reduce street violence and save countless lives.

The message is one that all of us can benefit from. I have no idea what the future holds for Stanley Williams. But I do know that he is taking advantage of the present to make a difference. This is something that all of us can do.

Message!

People can and often do change, which is one reason we should never give up on anyone. Stanley Williams might be the exception, but consider what could happen if every gang member had a mentor or benefactor who showed them a better way.

THOSE HYPOCRITES

In his informative and exciting book, *Discovering Your North Star,* Dr. Ike Reighard identifies a hypocrite in this fashion. He says, "In the Roman theater, the cast of actors was all male. To play the role of women, or perhaps to play the role of anyone who looked quite different from themselves, they put on a mask. This was called 'playing a hypocrite.' The word *hypocrite* used to mean only that a person wore a temporary mask to play a part in a play. It has come to mean 'phony' or 'pretending to be better than we are.'"

Dr. Reighard points out, "We experience tremendous stress in trying to be somebody we're not. It is like trying to hold balloons under water. We may be able to wrestle one or two beneath the surface, but sooner or later, one pops up . . . usually with intensity! In the same way, eventually our mask of the calm, competent person falls off, and the hurt and angry actual face is seen . . . but only for a moment before the mask is quickly put back on.

Here are some masks that people wear:

- We wear the mask of a hero, but we are afraid to fail.

- We wear the mask of a comedian to hide our hurt and to divert attention from harsh realities.

- We wear the mask of someone completely in control, because we are terrified of being out of control.

- We wear the mask of a nice, accommodating person, because we want to avoid conflict at all costs.

- We wear the mask of a person who never fails, because we only feel safe if everything goes perfectly.

- We wear the mask of a caring person, because we hope that will win appreciation from those we help.

- We wear the mask of an incompetent slob, because nobody expects much from somebody like that.

- We wear the mask of a rebel, because it makes people admire us from a distance.

- We wear the mask of rage, because we want people to be controlled by our anger.

- We wear the mask of a shy, withdrawn person, because most people won't hurt somebody who is so fragile."

Dr. Reighard points out that the stress of trying to be somebody we are not is a never-ending battle. I'm of the opinion that if you can't make it being yourself, you certainly can't make it being somebody else. It's OK to learn from others, even to discover some of the techniques or procedures they use in the process of becoming successful. But trying to be someone else really is hypocritical. Admire others; learn from others. But don't try to be somebody you're not.

> *"We are not hypocrites in our sleep."*
> **—William Hazlitt**

The other side of hypocrisy is consistency. When someone who doesn't know you personally asks questions of someone who knows you well on a personal and professional basis, their answers will speak volumes about you. The most popular question is invariably, "Is he or she really like he or she appears to be, or is the private person different from the public one?"

Question: When—not if—that question is asked about you, what will your friends be able to say with enthusiasm? If it's, "What you see is what you get," or something like, "Yes, he or she is true blue," you just passed the acid test. But if your friend has to smile and use doublespeak and deal in generalities, I encourage you to take a fresh look at who you are. Resolve to become the kind of person who always gets an enthusiastic thumbs-up endorsement.

I believe if you'll pay careful attention to what Dr. Reighard had to say and take these additional thoughts to heart, it will make a significant difference in your life.

Message!

It's true that truth can be denied, but it can't be avoided. Sooner or later you will be found out. So play it straight. You'll be glad you did.

——— 54 ———
ORIGINAL DIAGNOSIS

"The greatest obstacle to your success is probably you."
—Frank Tyger

When I was a youngster, I would hear someone make a statement about another person in southern slang: "He just ain't no 'count," or "He will never amount to a hill of beans," indicating that in their opinion the person in question had no future. But history has proven that many times those early opinions were ill-founded and wrong.

My younger brother wanted to follow me into sales, but he did not have the "touch." Though he struggled mightily, he just couldn't sell. He persisted and ultimately broke not only my sales records but company records as well.

An exciting story in *Investor's Business Daily* by Nancy Gondo about Louis Braille is a classic example of how we often feel that a "handicapped" person has no future. But the disability simply requires them to do things in a different way. As a three-year-old, Louis Braille, who had been forbidden to touch his father's tools, climbed up on a work-bench and picked up a sharp metal awl to poke holes in leather. Tragically, the awl slipped and plunged into his left eye. As a result, Louis developed an eye infection that spread to his other eye. This caused total blindness by the time he was four years old.

In the early nineteenth century, to be blind was to be helpless and forever dependent on others. Fortunately, his parents did not buy that idea, and they decided not to treat Louis differently from his siblings. Louis was a persistent youngster. He used the cane his father made him to memorize how many taps it took to get from one point to another. He developed a keen sense of smell and identity with sounds. At age six a local priest tutored him three times a week. He had a marvelous memory and was able to memorize the names of writers and artists, and could recite long verses of poetry.

Because of Braille's keen mind, the priest prevailed on the village schoolmaster to take him as a student, and Louis soaked up everything. With his mental alertness, he could solve complex math problems in his head. But he could not read and write. He could only sit and listen to turning pages.

When Louis was about ten, Charles Barbier, a retired ship's captain, had developed a code system of raised dots and dashes in heavy paper so French soldiers could send messages in the dark. In 1821 he offered his "sonography" method to blind students. Louis was ecstatic, finding it easy to read dots and dashes with his fingers and writing messages using a stylus on paper. The problem was that the system was based on sounds, so there were no numbers or punctuation marks. As a result, Louis spent all of his free time working to simplify the groups of dots and dashes.

> "We do not meet with success except by reiterated efforts."
> —*Françoise de Maintenon*

Barbier's system used as many as twenty dots per syllable and up to one hundred per word. It took him many months, but Louis Braille dramatically simplified the system. His school arranged for him to meet Barbier, who left insulted that a thirteen-year-old youth was suggesting changes to his method. Braille persisted, though, and by age fifteen his system was completed and is still in use today.

In our church there is a very bright young woman, Sandra Spoonemore, who gets around in a motorized wheelchair. She's a tiny girl, but her intellect and attitude are outstanding. She recently returned from Australia, where she was recognized for her creativity in her field. As a business consultant, she is making significant contributions to society, despite her "handicap." In 2000 she was a recipient of the

Dallas Mayor's Committee for the Employment of People with Disabilities Millennium Citizenship Award.

Question: Just what is a hill of beans worth, anyway?

Message!

You are the determining factor in your future. Don't let others be your judge and jury with their pity and negative thoughts or feeling. Know that you are here for a reason. Recognize, develop, and use the resources you do have. Others see the surface; you know your heart.

—— *55* ——

SEVENTEEN RULES
OF LIFE

"Wisdom is knowing what to do next, virtue is doing it."
—*David Starr Jordan*

For many years there has been speculation about the beliefs of the founding fathers of the United States. George Washington wrote the following "rules of life" while still a schoolboy. We commend them to you since they are said to have sustained and guided, and finally brought to ultimate victory, the first president of our land:

1. Act at all times as in the presence of God and make it the great object in all things to please him. In order to do this:

2. Seek first of all to gain clear views of his will and with regard to all things, to be perfectly conformed to it. In doing this:

3. Cherish no thoughts, indulge no feelings, speak no words and do no actions but what you really think after all the

light you can gain will most honor God, most benefit yourself and others, and give you the greatest joy when they come to be exhibited before the assembled universe at the judgment day.

4. Begin and end each day by a season of communion with God and by a solemn and hearty commitment of yourself and all your interests, temporal and eternal, to his guidance, care and disposal.

5. Daily read with deep attention and fervent prayer a portion of the word of God for the purpose of understanding, believing and obeying it.

6. Never express or indulge the least degree of unkindness toward any human being and give no needless pain to anyone of the human race or even of the animal creation.

7. Make it your object to promote the greatest happiness of the whole of all upon whom you may have influence both of the present and all future generations.

8. Regard the hand of God in all the dispensations of his providence and in whatsoever state he places you therewith be content.

9. Envy none who are above you, and despise none who are below you, but possess and manifest the utmost good will toward all men.

10. Never speak of any or feel toward them in a manner that you ought not to wish them under similar circumstances to speak or feel with regard to you.

11. Let all statements and narrations be an exact exhibition of the real Truth.

12. Act for God, for the universe and for eternity and in such a manner as is adopted to promote the highest good forever. In order to do this:

13. Look habitually to Jesus Christ. Let your whole soul be imbued with his spirit and manifest it in all your actions.

"Wisdom denotes the pursuing of the best ends by the best means."
—Frances Hutcheson

14. Look to the Holy Ghost as the author of all good in man. Seek habitually his teaching, his illuminating and purifying influences that he may dwell in you as his temple and take full possession of all your powers and talents for him.

15. Earnestly desire that he would take of the things of Christ and more and more show them unto you and carefully avoid everything which tends to hinder you from becoming perfectly like him.

16. Make it as your meat and drink to do the will of God and perseveringly have respect to all his commandments.

17. Feel and acknowledge that all the good that you ever have received, that you now receive, or ever will receive is of grace through Jesus Christ. Trust in him for all which you need, both for this life and the life to come. Rely on his

merits, imitate his example and in view of every blessing give him, and the Father and the Holy Ghost, all the glory.

—George Washington

I believe these rules are indicative of most, if not all, of our founding fathers. I am confident that all of them were men of honesty, courage, character, faith, and integrity. Their love of freedom and country was consistently demonstrated throughout their lives. The young George Washington voiced the ideal that the other founding fathers embraced.

Message!

George Washington gave us all an example that, when followed, will bring honor to God, self, and fellowman.

— 56 —
AMERICA THE BEAUTIFUL

I love America because we are a compassionate land. If there is an earthquake in India or Turkey, Americans are the first there with the most aid. If there is a typhoon in the Philippines, Americans are there first to render aid. If there is a famine in Afghanistan, even as we bombed that land in response to the terrorist attacks, we were also flying in food to the starving. Even before the war started, America gave more aid to Afghanistan than did any other nation. If there is a drought in Africa, floods in Central America, poverty in Haiti or Somalia, or ethnic cleansing in the Balkans, America and Americans are there to help.

We are a haven for asylum seekers from all over the world. Millions of immigrants apply every year to enter our land. Once they become citizens, these immigrants, regardless of where they come from, are four times as likely to become millionaires as are those who are born here. In short, they take advantage of the opportunities America offers. I love America because it's not where you start that counts.

I love America because despite what some say, historical evidence is absolutely irrefutable that we were founded as a Christian nation, although we have strayed away from those roots. Now, largely thanks to the terrorists and that September 11, 2001, wake-up call, we have returned to our roots. In the early part of the nineteenth century, Alexis de Tocqueville from France said he had seen everything America has to offer, but it wasn't until he went into the churches that he discovered America's greatness. His conclusion was that America is great because America is good, and America will be great as long as it is good. We've moved back in the right direction. We are now on God's side. It never was a question of whether or not he was on our side. He is always on the right side.

I love America because of what it has permitted me to do and become. I was the tenth of twelve children. My dad died when I was five; my mother had a fifth-grade education. But because of the concern and help so many people have given me throughout my life, I count twenty-six men and women whose photos appear on my "Wall of Gratitude." Their help, love, and encouragement have enabled me to become successful in my chosen career and in my personal and family life beyond what anyone could reasonably expect.

I love America because of its great diversity. The six people who had the most impact on my life were all women, and minorities have played a huge part in my life. Three American Indians were critically important to my journey, one in my sales career, another in my speaking career, and yet another in my spiritual life. I'm a Christian because an elderly black woman spent a weekend in our home on July 4, 1972. My daughter-in-law is from Campeche, Mexico. Our director of international operations and product development is from India. I'm the spokesperson for Nikken, a large Japanese company with a Korean president.

Interestingly, DNA now proves that Adam and Eve really did start it all. Acts 17:26 says that we are all "one blood." My closest friend (he is more like a brother) for the last thirty-seven years is a Jew from Winnipeg, Canada. My favorite writers are Jews—David, Solomon, Matthew, Mark, Paul, etc. I shudder to think what my life would have been like had I been sexist or racist.

I love America because of people like Oprah Winfrey, who was born to a single mother, raised in poverty in Mississippi, sexually abused by relatives, gave birth as a young girl and overcame all of these things to positively influence people all over the world. Mary Kay Ash started her great company on a shoestring and built it on the philosophy that God comes first, family second, and Mary Kay Cosmetics third in the lives of her representatives. Her pink Cadillacs, won by literally thousands of her directors all over the world, are shining lights of opportunity. Mary Crowley founded Home Interiors and Gifts and gave opportunities to countless people through her charitable efforts, literally rescued several Christian colleges, and provided scholarships for thousands of deserving young men and women. These three women have enriched the lives of millions of people and been responsible for billions of dollars in our economy.

I love America because we are a nation of laws.

I love America because a black lady, Rosa Parks, refused to leave her seat in the front of a bus and move to the back with the simple statement, "My feet hurt." As a result, the boycott in Montgomery, Alabama, was on and Martin Luther King's crusade for civil rights caught fire. When Rosa Parks refused to stand up and move back, an entire people stood up and moved forward—that's America.

Most of all, I love America because of the freedom she offers. This is not to say that America is perfect. But of all the nations on the face of this earth, this is the one that offers the most opportunity to those who are willing to obey the laws, go to work, and do their best.

Yes, I love America because I can tell a thousand stories of men and women of every race, creed, and color, with every physical handicap you can possibly imagine who have taken the resources they had and because of their faith, friends, families, and freedoms, have accomplished great things and made a difference in the lives of countless other people. Yes, I love America because it truly is the "land of the free and the home of the brave," the land where any man or woman has an opportunity to do great things, and most of all to enjoy the privilege of freedom.

It really is "America the beautiful," and I hope you will do your part to help keep her that way.

suggesting, and you will become a happier, healthier, friendlier, better person.

Message!

If you are somebody to anybody, you are somebody. When you accept the fact that you are somebody, you will find it easy to treat others as "somebody" too.

—— 50 ——
THE PRIVILEGES
OF "GET TO"

"The key to whatever success I enjoy today is: Don't ask. Do."
—Vikki Carr

When you woke up this morning, were your thoughts on what you've "got to do" or what you "get to do"? If your thoughts were on what you've "got to do," they can be either negative or positive. For example, if you've "got to go to work," that's positive because it means you have a job and are gainfully employed. Not only that, you have a means of getting to your place of employment and you have the health and energy to do exactly that. So your "got to" is translated into positive steps toward performing what you "get to do" because at the end of the work period you "get to" cash your paycheck. Then you "get to" use that money to pay bills. Some of it will go to buy food, clothing, and shelter, and, ideally, a part of it will go to your church or favorite charity as well as to your retirement plan.

By and large, however, when we think of "got to," we think of something that we are required to do whether we want to do it or not. For example, we've "got to" make those car and house payments; we've "got to" be on time or risk losing our job; we've "got to" perform satisfactorily or be dismissed; we've "got to" get home at a certain time to prepare the evening meal for our family; we've "got to" make those phone calls we've been neglecting; we've "got to" visit an elderly relative who is in a nursing home or hospital; we've "got to . . . got to . . . got to. . . ."

If we concentrate on the particular line of thought of what we've "got to" do, we're probably going to have a stressful day and end it by being tired and perhaps even a little "out of sorts."

I love the "get to" approach that Lesleigh Ann Schaefer describes. She shares with her Internet readers how at age forty-four she went back to college and is now headed for graduation. She made a list of her "get to's," which will give all of us something to think about:

- I get to go to school to fulfill my dream.
- I get to go to work when so many people can't.
- I get to do the laundry, thankful for a washer and dryer.
- I get to play with my cat who is so thankful for the attention.

- I get to say a prayer; I have freedom of speech.
- I get to remember the things that make me happy.
- I get to spend time with a friend who needs my help.
- I get to read a book; I still have my sight.

Lesleigh Ann's is a spirit and attitude that contributes not only to her physical and financial well-being but also to her emotional and social well-being as well.

"No great man ever complains of want of opportunity."
—Ralph Waldo Emerson

Suggestions: Take out your pen and paper and begin to make a list, eliminating your "got to's" and concentrating entirely on your "get to's." "I get to visit my mother in the nursing home," "I get to make a phone call to cheer up a friend who is confined to her home," "I get to write that thank-you note to someone who sent me a nice remembrance on Valentine's Day," "I get to read that book I've been wanting to read on how to get a raise," "I get to clean out my garage and make it more attractive in case unexpected opportunities to sell my home develop, so that I can reduce my costs of living and get to enjoy life more." Let your imagination run full bore. List all of the things you are grateful you get to do. It is amazing how much more excitement will be generated when you concentrate on the "get to's" of life.

positions him or her for higher education and a successful career in business. When you learn how to do your own job properly, that puts you in position to teach someone else how to do the same job. And the way you move up the ladder, in most cases, is to be replacing yourself constantly—teaching, training, and inspiring others.

"To be loved, be lovable."
—Ovid

It works in your personal life, as well. The relationships you have with your family will put you in a position to have either a great attitude when you leave the house and prepare you for effectiveness on the job, or it could give you a lousy attitude and you might arrive in a bad mood. That takes you out of position to do your best work that day.

Everything builds on everything else. The words you say, the actions you take, the attitudes you develop, your friendliness, your spirit of cooperation and team play—all add up to putting you in a great position to continue to make progress in all areas of your life, or could take you out of the game. The thought should be, _What effect will this have on others?_ When you think about it just for a moment, you can get in the habit of being the right kind of person—which puts you in position to do the right thing, which enables you to get more of the things life has to offer.

Message!

Every step or move you make has an impact on your future. That's why you should weigh each step like the chess masters do—by carefully considering what will happen down the road as a result of your next move.

——— 46 ———

ENCOURAGING OTHERS HELPS YOU

I want to tell you about something that happened immediately thereafter as a direct result of what the participants learned in one of our special two-day "Born to Win" seminars.

When someone makes a contribution at "Born to Win," we encourage the others to write him or her a little note of encouragement on our "I like . . . because" pads. After this seminar was over, a group of eleven participants, including Gina Womack, who at that time was our associate support manager, went to the Trail Dust Steakhouse for dinner. Gina reported that they had a really neat waitress named Wendy who provided them with excellent service.

> *"I think no innocent species of wit or pleasantry should be suppressed; and that a good pun may be admitted among the smaller excellencies of lively conversation."*
> **—James Boswell**

After the orders were taken, the group was visiting and having a wonderful time swapping stories when one of the gentlemen, Peter Tricklebank from Australia, suggested they write an "I like . . . because" for Wendy. Since they had none of the forms with them, they improvised by using a napkin. Peter wrote his name and next to it wrote what he liked about Wendy. Then he passed it on to the others and one by one each participant wrote specific, observable behavior he or she liked about Wendy. The napkin was completely covered, front and back, and in addition each person attached his or her business card.

At the end of the meal the group asked Wendy to come back to the table. When she did, according to Gina, they presented her with the napkin and, to quote Gina, "The biggest smile I have ever seen spread across her face. She simply glowed." At that point, Gina said, they applauded Wendy for a good three minutes. All she could do was smile and laugh with sheer delight. On the way out, several people hugged her and thanked her for her outstanding service. "She was in tears as we were walking out the door. Once we were outside," according to Gina, "we were all incredibly pumped and full of excitement, talking about how incredible it felt and how powerful words are."

Gina said she assured everyone that Wendy would not remember the night before or the night after, but she